How Much Is Enough?

30 Days to Personal Revival

LARRY BURKETT
with Kay Moore

ISBN 0-7673-9559-X

Dewey Decimal Classification: 248.6
Subject Heading: STEWARDSHIP\DEVOTIONAL LITERATURE

Printed in the United States of America

Church Stewardship Services
LifeWay Christian Resources
127 Ninth Avenue, North
Nashville, TN 37234

Table of Contents

Ideation Team

David T. Button, Lou Ann Cave — *International Mission Board*

Barbara J. Elder — *Woman's Missionary Union*

Curtis D. Sharp — *Annuity Board*

Bob Lee Franklin — *North American Mission Board*

Clarence E. Hackett, William F. Montgomery — *Florida Baptist Convention*

Rodney J. Wiltrout — *California Baptist State Convention*

David A. Michel — *Mississippi Baptist State Convention*

John D. MacLaren — *Alabama Baptist State Convention*

Kay Moore — *Author*

Larry Burkett, Sam B. Conway, Michael E. Taylor — *Christian Financial Concepts*

Gary L. Aylor, Donnie E. Baldwin, J. David Carter, J. David Chamberlain, Belvin Cox, John H. Franklin, Norma J. Goldman, Ed Summers — *LifeWay Christian Resources*

Production Team

Gene Mims, *Vice President, LifeWay Christian Leadership*
Michael D. Miller, *Director, LifeWay Church Leadership*
Gary L. Aylor, *Director, Church Stewardship Services*
Norma J. Goldman, *Editorial Team Leader*
Linda W. Grammer, *Assistant Editor*

Foreword

It is amazing what God will do when we ask! When we considered our assignment in stewardship education, we asked ourselves two specific questions. "What can we do with limited human resources to make a significant impact on believers in the area of lifestyle stewardship? How can we redefine stewardship so that it can be understood in today's world the way it is described in the Bible?" We asked, because this is our passion and our calling.

We believe that God led us through every step in the development of *How Much Is Enough? 30 Days to Personal Revival.* We believe without a doubt that *all of our partners in the venture,* and our association with Larry Burkett and Kay Moore, are of God. We humbly and gratefully acknowledge the support and encouragement of our friend and leader, Dr. James T. Draper, Jr.

We affirm the power of the Holy Spirit to remold and shape us so that we stand in sharp contrast to the world system — a system that recognizes neither personal accountability, nor the Lordship of Jesus Christ.

It is our joyful expectation and prayer that you, dear student of the Word, will be changed, encouraged, helped and led to a deeply satisfying and rich experience of blessing as you align your identity, priorities, values and habits with His!

Gary L. Aylor, *Director, Church Stewardship Services*
J. David Carter, *Lead Stewardship Specialist*
Norma J. Goldman, *Editorial Team Leader*

Covenant

As you participate in *How Much Is Enough? 30 Days to Personal Revival,* you are asked to dedicate yourself to God and to your *How Much Is Enough?* small group by making several commitments. Right now, you may not be able to do everything listed, but by signing this covenant, you pledge to adopt these practices as you progress through the study.

As a disciple of Jesus Christ, I commit myself to —

- Acknowledge Jesus Christ as Lord of my life each day;
- Attend all group sessions unless providentially hindered;
- Spend the time necessary to complete my daily assignments;
- Have a daily quiet time;
- Be faithful to my church in attendance and in stewardship of everything entrusted to my care;
- Love and encourage each member of my group;
- Share my faith with others;
- Keep in strict confidence anything shared by others in the group sessions;
- Willingly submit myself to others in matters of accountability;
- Become a discipler of others as God gives opportunities;
- Support my church financially by practicing biblical giving; and
- Pray daily for group members.

(You may wish to list the names of your small group members in the space provided so that you can pray for them daily.)

_____ _____

_____ _____

_____ _____

_____ _____

_____ _____

Signed:_____ Date:_____

How Much
Is Enough?

Devotional
Week 1, Day 1

This Week's Lessons

Memory Verse

"For you created my inmost being; you knit me together in my mother's womb. I praise you because I am fearfully and wonderfully made."

-Psalm 139:13-14

What Is the Source of My Identity?

"For you created my inmost being; you knit me together in my mother's womb. I praise you because I am fearfully and wonderfully made . . . ." (Psalm 139: 13-14)

It is nearly impossible to function in the American culture without personal identification. You can't board a commercial airliner without a photo ID. Signing up your child for pee-wee soccer requires a notarized birth certificate. Even writing a personal check requires a valid form of identification. You must prove who you are.

It is even more essential for Christians to have a clear understanding of our identity in Christ in order to effectively serve Him. Powerful cultural forces, however, complicate our ability to understand who we are and why we are here on this earth. People commonly think of themselves in light of the roles they play in life. "Who are you?" "Why, I'm a banker," or "I'm the mother of four children," or "I'm Cynthia's husband."

An even more subtle temptation is to define ourselves by the amount of "things" we can acquire. We've come to equate importance with living in a large home on the fashionable side of town, driving a particular model car, or wearing name-brand clothing. The great danger of defining ourselves by temporal things is that they eventually fade away. Take away the nice things, and who are we?

Thankfully, a careful reading of Psalm 139:13-16 reveals some lasting truths about who we are as God's children. First, note God's involvement in our creation. The apostle Paul writes in Ephesians 1:4 that *"He chose us in him before the creation of the world."* God has patiently waited for your arrival on the scene because you have unique contributions to make to life!

Week 1

Day 1

Devotional *continued...*

Further, King David remarks that we are *"fearfully and wonderfully made"* (Psalm 139:14). By putting a premium on beauty or on brute strength, our culture creates an artificial standard that is hopelessly beyond what most of us can achieve. Perhaps *you* sometimes feel like a second-class person because you can't measure up to those standards. But God made no mistake in your creation. And He delights in variety — red, tall, brown, small, yellow, large, black, petite, or white. Stewardship of your life begins at the point of being thankful for the unique way God created you! Does praise to God or resentment describe your response to the way He has created you?

Perhaps the deepest insight into the identity that we find from God is the discovery of His plan for our lives. *"All the days ordained for me were written in your book before one of them came to be"* (Psalm 139:16). Faithful stewardship involves deliberately using all the resources entrusted to us by God, including time, in order to fulfill His purposes for our lives. Ultimately, the meaning and satisfaction we experience in our lives results from living for Him.

As you contemplate your identity in Christ, consider this. Does your lifestyle prove beyond a reasonable doubt that you belong to the Lord Jesus Christ?

Interactive — Week 1, Day 1

How did you feel when you just read the precious reminder about you from
Ephesians 1:4: "He chose us in him before the creation of the world"?
(Check one.)

_____a. Who, me? I'm not worthy. I'm sure I'm not that important to God.
_____b. That's impossible. How could God actually know and care about
         individual people?
_____c. I'd like to believe that's true, but I have lots of doubts.
_____d. Wow! What an awesome reminder! Thank You, God, that You
         planned for me all along. I feel very special!

You are truly worthy! God loved you before you ever were. What greater identity
could you have than this? I sincerely hope you were able to check the last sentence.

What cultural standards intimidate you? Fill in the blanks with words or phrases
that indicate how you sometimes feel you don't measure up.

I wish I were _____. I'm unhappy with myself
because I don't own _____. If I only could
achieve _____, I'd be satisfied. Things would be
just fine if I looked _____.

What you achieve or own doesn't determine who you are. Even without the temporal things you listed, you have a unique identity in Christ. You are a person of
worth because He says so!

What are some of the unique contributions you have to make to life? Below, list
what you think some of those are.

_____

_____

You may have written something like this: *I am a good listener. I try to minister to
neighbors who are sick. I teach my children God's truths, etc.* Unlike possessions or
accomplishments, these kinds of investments in God's Kingdom are things that last.

Do you believe that you are genuinely thankful for the unique way God created
you?

❑ Yes   ❑ No

Interactive — Week 1, Day 1

If you answered no, what kind of an attitude change would be necessary so you could have a thankful spirit for who you are?

_____

_____

_____

You might need to spend more time in God's Word to help jump-start a spirit of thankfulness. Or, fellowshipping with believers who affirm you also can help renew a grateful heart. Resolve to remind yourself every day that you are fearfully and wonderfully made!

Below, write out a brief prayer of praise to God for creating you just the way you are.

_____

_____

_____

Psalm 139:16 reminds you that God knows how you use the resources He has entrusted to you and what kind of steward you are of these. Which words below describe how you feel when you realize this? (Check all that apply.)

❑ a. embarrassed   ❑ e. terrified

❑ b. satisfied   ❑ f. disappointed

❑ c. apathetic   ❑ g. worried

❑ d. joyful   ❑ h. other _____

Below, give an example of how the use of your resources demonstrates that you belong to Christ.

_____

_____

_____

If you believe you have some room for growth in this area, you're not alone. In the days ahead, you'll learn more about how to honor Christ more with this part of your life.

Devotional
Week 1, Day 2

Memory Verse

"Whoever has my commands and obeys them, he is the one who loves me. He who loves me will be loved by my Father, and I too will love him and show myself to him."

-John 14:21

Does the Time I Spend in the Word Reflect Who I Am in Christ?

"Whoever has my commands and obeys them, he is the one who loves me. He who loves me will be loved by my Father, and I too will love him and show myself to him." (John 14:21)

It is estimated that America's 100 million households will have over 200 billion pieces of mail delivered in 1999 — an average of 2,000 items per year, nearly 40 pieces per week! Most of it is junk mail. But what about receiving a personal, hand-addressed envelope? Now that's intriguing, especially if the letter is from a loved one.

Think of the Bible as God's personal love letter to you. In it, He reveals His hopes and will for you. God recounts His mighty deeds in days past to build your confidence in His faithfulness. He also reveals His standard of holy behavior so you will know how to express your love to Him through obedience. Most of all, the Bible reveals His great love for you. *"For as high as the heavens are above the earth, so great is his love for those who fear him"* (Psalm 103:11). You will truly begin to live freely when you realize you can never earn more of His love; you can only receive it and learn to relax in the security of it!

Do you struggle to maintain a consistent effort in Bible study? Perhaps you've never been trained to study the Bible devotionally. For instance, can you name anyone who has ever spent time with you, one on one, showing you how to study the Bible? Are you now proficient enough to train someone else — perhaps your children, a new Christian, or even your neighbor?

Week 1
Day 2

Devotional *continued...*

How strong is your conviction to study God's Word? You know you should, but you just lack the power to remain consistent. If that's the case, rather than playing games with God or wallowing around in guilt, I suggest you confess your lack of commitment to the Lord and ask Him to rekindle a fresh, vibrant love for Him in your heart. A sentence prayer won't do. Instead, you may need to cry out to God in prayer and fasting for a time, while you seek Him in Bible study. Concentrate on the life of Jesus or read the Psalms for starters.

A recent survey by the Barna Research Group, Ltd. reveals that 91 percent of American households have at least one Bible! That's great; God's "love letter" is well distributed. Another 80 percent regard the Bible as the most influential book in human history; that's even better. People hold the Bible in high regard, but only 38 percent of Americans actually *read* the Bible at least once a week, not including while at church.[1]

What does the amount of time you spend in God's Word say about your devotion to Him? Is His Word received like junk mail or like a love letter specifically for you?

[1] www.barna.org/PageStats.htm (8/5/98)

Interactive — Week 1, Day 2

Part of being a good steward of God's resources means spending time in His Word. Do you have a consistent, daily quiet time for this purpose?

❑ Yes   ❑ No

If yes, what time of day is it? _____ a.m. _____ p.m.
Where are you when it occurs? _____
    (office, bedroom, study, den, breakfast room, etc.)
What materials do you have with you? _____
_____
    (commentaries, devotional guides, journals, etc.)
What type of setting generally helps you study the Bible most effectively?
_____
    (outdoors, indoors, solitude, moderate activity nearby, religious music playing, etc.)

What is your biggest stumbling block to maintaining a daily quiet time?

❑   I wait too late, until the end of the day, to begin.
❑   I don't see the need for one.
❑   I fail to prioritize my time efficiently.
❑   I don't like repetition.
❑   I'm just too busy.
❑   Other _____

If you spent no time with a friend, your spouse, or your neighbor, you would know little about that person. Similarly, you can make excuses, but the bottom line is, you will know little of God and of His purposes for you unless you spend time in His Word.

Psalm 42:1-2 describes a thirst for God. Can you describe a time in which you can remember having a distinct longing to know God through His Word, like a thirsty person might long for a drink of water?

_____
_____
_____

Interactive — Week 1, Day 2

The second paragraph of this Devotional lists things that God does for you through the Bible — His personal love letter to you. Below, check the one that has benefited you most in a recent circumstance. Then describe how you experienced that benefit.

- ❑ He reveals His hopes and will for you.
- ❑ He recounts His mighty deeds in days past to build your confidence and faithfulness.
- ❑ He reveals His standard of holy behavior so you will know how to express your love to Him through obedience.
- ❑ He reveals His great love for you.
- ❑ He reveals His great plan for your life.

_____

_____

_____

_____

Are you satisfied with the *quality* of your daily quiet time spent in God's Word?

❑ Yes   ❑ No

If not, describe one specific thing you could do to improve the quality of that time.

_____

_____

_____

_____

You might have answered: *I could turn off the television an hour earlier at night to devote to a quiet time. I could ask my spouse to be an accountability partner for me. I could locate a translation of the Bible that really relates to me.*

God has given you time to use wisely. I hope that at the end of each day, you can say your best stewardship of His time has included a period of exploring His Word.

Devotional
Week 1, Day 3

Memory Verse

"The prayer of a righteous man is powerful and effective."

-James 5:16

Does the Time I Spend in Prayer Reflect Who I Am in Christ?

"The prayer of a righteous man is powerful and effective." (James 5:16)

If God didn't hear your prayers, there really would be no reason to pray, would there? Praying would simply degenerate into an exercise of spiritual futility — nothing more than a lame attempt at self-righteousness. Or, if God did hear but didn't care, there still would be no reason to pray. Why would you bother pouring your heart out to a brick wall? Or suppose that God did hear and care, but He was utterly powerless to answer?

But thankfully, none of that is true. The testimony of Scripture is that God not only hears your prayers, but He is incredibly interested in the details of your life. *"You know when I sit and when I rise; you perceive my thoughts from afar . . . . Before a word is on my tongue you know it completely, O Lord"* (Psalm 139:2,4). Because of your righteous standing through the shed blood of Jesus Christ, God not only hears your prayers, He delights at the sound of your voice!

Not only does God hear, but His compassion defies measure. *"The Lord is close to the brokenhearted and saves those who are crushed in spirit"* (Psalm 34:18). Rather than a cold and impersonal machine, God is deeply touched by your petitions. When you grieve, He grieves. When you rejoice, He rejoices with you. To be compassionate is to be like Him, because He is the epitome of compassion.

He hears, He cares, and, yes, He answers prayer. Just ask Moses and the Israelites who cried out to God as Pharaoh's chariots bore down upon them (Exodus 14:10). Or read the answer to Elijah's prayer during the

Week 1

Day 3

Devotional *continued...*

showdown with the prophets of Baal (1 Kings 18:37). And I wonder what Rhoda would say about prayer after Peter's miraculous deliverance from prison; of course, it was during a fervent prayer meeting at the church (Acts 12:5-14). You get the picture: *powerful* and *effective.* That's how the Word of God describes the prayers of righteous people. Circumstances change. Attitudes change. *You* will change. The impossible and unexpected comes to pass.

The great prayer warrior, S. D. Gordon, once stated, "The greatest thing anyone can do for God and man is pray. It is not the *only* thing, but it is the *chief* thing. The great people of the earth today are the people who pray. I do not mean those who talk about prayer, nor those who say they believe in prayer, nor yet those who can explain about prayer; but I mean those people who take time to pray."[1]

The question is, how much are you missing in your Christian life simply because you've become discouraged or lazy in prayer? Don't believe Satan's lies that God doesn't hear, care, or answer your prayers. Instead, He anxiously waits to hear from you. Spiritual transactions will be left undone unless you meet with Him.

[1] Dick Eastman, *Change the World School of Prayer Manual* (Studio City: World Literature Crusade, 1976), iv.

Interactive — Week 1, Day 3

In its first paragraph, this Devotional lists three of Satan's lies about prayer. Which of these statements have you ever found yourself thinking? (Check all that apply.)

- ❏ God doesn't hear my prayers.
- ❏ He hears but doesn't care.
- ❏ He hears and cares but is powerless to answer.

Hopefully, you have also experienced God's truth that counters these lies — the fact that God truly is involved with your life's specifics.

Can you recall a time in which you have seen how God, through answered prayer, has shown you just how concerned He is with the details of your life? If so, describe it below.

_____

_____

_____

You might have described a time when God helped you work out transportation arrangements to travel home from college, or provided a Christian friend for you, or helped you discover a way to pay your bills. Yes, God is even available to help you learn to be a good financial steward. He eagerly involves Himself in those details, too! Whatever your own personal story is, you can surely testify to God's specific provision, again and again!

Reread S. D. Gordon's quote about prayer being "not the only thing" but the "chief thing" in life. Has there been a time in your life when you prayed about a matter only after you exhausted all other efforts?

❏ Yes   ❏ No

If you answered "Yes," describe the situation.

_____

_____

_____

All of us have sometimes used prayer as the last recourse instead of the first. God wants to be our first resort, at all times.

Interactive — Week 1, Day 3

You may genuinely want to take time to pray but need some how-tos. You wonder. *What does God want me to pray about?* Although prayers don't need a specific formula, some guidelines help. Try the following, for practice.

Think of one thing for which you desire to thank God. Write a one or two-sentence prayer doing just that. *Example: Thank You, Lord, for helping me get to work safely today.*

_____

_____

_____

Now, praise Him for Who He is — for aspects of His character. *Example: Lord, I praise You for being omniscient — for knowing everything about me, yet loving me anyway.*

_____

_____

_____

Confess your sins. Psalm 66:18 says "If I had cherished sin in my heart, the Lord would not have listened." *Example: Father, forgive me for failing to be content with what I have.*

_____

_____

_____

Ask for what you need (petition); pray for others (intercession). *Examples: Lord, help me know how to answer this difficult letter. Help my brother find a job to provide for his family.*

_____

_____

_____

Wise stewardship of your time involves communicating with God regularly. When you pray, you partner with Him in what He wants to accomplish in your life and in the world.

Devotional
Week 1, Day 4

Memory Verse

"I have no greater joy than to hear that my children are walking in the truth."

-3 John 4

How Does the Time I Spend with My Family Reflect Who I Am in Christ?

"I have no greater joy than to hear that my children are walking in the truth."
(3 John 4)

The banging on the hotel door startled me from my sleep. My wife Judy and I were in Chattanooga, Tennessee where I was teaching a Christian Business Men's Conference. I stumbled to the door to find Dr. Ted DeMoss, the president of CBMC.

"Larry, you've got a call downstairs at the front desk. It's a hospital in Atlanta and they say it's urgent." Needless to say, I scrambled for clothes and hurried to take the call. An emergency room nurse quickly explained that my son Dan had been involved in a serious automobile accident, and the doctors had to operate to save his life.

"Hurry," she said.

Judy and I threw our things into the car and headed straight for Atlanta. During the two-hour drive, Dan's spiritual condition dominated my thoughts. Though he said he was a Christian, he wasn't living for the Lord, and I was sincerely concerned that he wasn't saved at all. All the way down I-75 I fervently prayed to God to spare him long enough for me to lead him to Christ. Dan survived, but the doctors painted a grim picture for us. Following surgery, he slipped into a deep coma and remained that way for the next seventy-nine days.

As you might imagine, I had a great deal of time to think about Dan during this time, and I continued to wonder if he would go to heaven if

Week 1
Day 4

Devotional *continued...*

he died. So, even though he couldn't respond, we read Scripture to him and played Christian music for him. With one of my family members teetering at death's door, eternal issues came into focus. I suspect it would be that way for you, too. Only one thing matters: Will you see this person again in eternity with Christ? By God's grace, Dan did recover, and I am pleased to report that he loves God and serves Him as a born-again Christian.

But here's my point. There are literally thousands of things to teach children about life — everything from how to tie a shoe to how to drive a car. There are academic lessons. There are culturally-appropriate manners. In all your teaching, don't minimize the most important lesson of all: how to come to salvation in Jesus Christ.

Don't make the mistake of providing money, toys, vacations, nice homes, cars, and even college educations to your children and neglect the gift that will last eternally: a personal knowledge of Jesus Christ. Don't wait for a near tragedy to bring this issue into focus like I did. Even if you're single or married without children, don't go to heaven alone. Find someone to take with you! You are a steward of your relationships. The apostle Paul was so close to Timothy that he calls him *"Timothy, my true son in the faith"* (1 Timothy 1:2).

Is anyone headed to heaven because of your influence? Obeying the Great Commission begins with you.

Interactive — Week 1, Day 4

What things do you believe hinder you from spending time with family members? Describe below.

_____

_____

_____

You may have listed things such as too much overtime at the office, too many volunteer commitments, or inability to say no to other demands on your time. Maybe you don't get along with some members of your family and look for ways to avoid them.

Some of these obstacles may seem insurmountable. You may realize you are being a poor steward of your time where your family is concerned but feel hopeless and helpless to change.

Look up the following Scripture passages in your Bible: Philippians 4:13, Zechariah 4:6b, John 15:5. After reading them, write below what these passages say to you about overcoming obstacles to family time:

_____

_____

_____

We do not overcome obstacles by our own power but by God's power working in us. God can give you the wisdom to make changes that will help you re-prioritize so your family can have more of your presence instead of tangible presents that you may believe are good substitutes.

What do your family members know about your spiritual life? Answer the questions below.

_____ is my favorite hymn.

_____ is my favorite Bible passage.

Here's where I was, how old I was, and what happened when I trusted Jesus as my Savior:

_____

_____

Interactive — Week 1, Day 4

Here's a way I've seen God at work in my life recently:

_____

_____

Now, spend some quality time with a family member. Go on a walk with your spouse, take your child out for a soft drink, visit a relative, etc. Share a couple of these facts with your loved one. Don't spend so much family time discussing trivia or schedules that you fail to talk about the crucial subject of your faith.

Think about your family members (including extended family.) Who among them, to your knowledge, does not have a personal relationship with Jesus Christ? Jot their initials on the line below.

_____

Does your heart break for these lost family members? Do you understand that you are a steward of these relationships? What are some things you can do to bear witness for Christ to your close relatives? Below, check any of these actions you will commit to take.

- ❏ Share with them a Christian book or other publication
- ❏ Invite them to go to church or to a religious program with you
- ❏ Demonstrate to them the fruit of the Spirit[1] and explain that Christ's love is the source of your actions
- ❏ Look for opportunities to tell about Christ
- ❏ Other _____

Stop and pray, asking God to open doors for you to share the gospel with those closest to you. Ask God to make you a good steward of your prayer time so that you will pray for unsaved relatives. Lift these up to the Throne of Grace frequently as you pray.

[1] Fruit of the Spirit is described in Galatians 5:22-23 as, *"love, joy, peace, patience, kindness, goodness, faithfulness, gentleness and self control."*

Devotional
Week 1, Day 5

Memory Verse

"What do you think? There was a man who had two sons. He went to the first and said, 'Son, go and work today in the vineyard.' 'I will not,' he answered, but later he changed his mind and went. Then the father went to the other son and said the same thing. He answered, 'I will, sir,' but he did not go. Which of the two did what his father wanted? 'The first,' they answered."

Matthew 21:28-31

Will Jesus Forgive My Stewardship Failures?

"What do you think? There was a man who had two sons. He went to the first and said, 'Son, go and work today in the vineyard.' 'I will not,' he answered, but later he changed his mind and went. Then the father went to the other son and said the same thing. He answered, 'I will, sir,' but he did not go. Which of the two did what his father wanted? 'The first,' they answered."

(Matthew 21:28-31)

We've looked at a series of challenging stewardship topics this week, including the source of your identity and your time in the Word, in prayer, and with your family. After careful introspection, the Holy Spirit may have guided you into areas that require growth and improvement. But will Jesus forgive you for past stewardship failures?

To a degree, I struggle with my eyesight. Without my glasses, everything is a blur. Similarly, when the apostle Paul tells us to *"Take the helmet of salvation and the sword of the Spirit, which is the word of God"* (Ephesians 6:17), he means that our thought patterns must be shaped through the lenses of the Word of God. Our salvation is the very helmet that protects our minds and thought patterns. Without salvation as a covering, our thoughts can go awry. Doubt creeps in.

This is particularly evident in the area of stewardship failures. We understand that, by grace, Jesus saves us from spiritual and moral sins. But we struggle to let go of stewardship failures like money management, spiritual disciplines, and family matters. Failures in these areas can have long-lasting effects, such as personal bankruptcy, divorce, and a lukewarm spirit.

Week 1
Day 5

Devotional *continued...*

Consider these three principles:

1. Jesus Christ died to forgive us of all sin. *"If we confess our sins, he is faithful and just and will forgive us our sins and purify us from all unrighteousness"* (1 John 1:9). Not from *some* or even *most* sin, He is faithful to purify us from *all* unrighteousness.

2. Once under the blood of Christ, dump the self-deprecation and negative attitudes. *"Therefore, there is now no condemnation for those who are in Christ Jesus"* (Romans 8:1). If Christ died for all your sins, why are you insistent on laboring under their weight? Rise up and walk!

3. Mismanagement of God's resources is not to be taken lightly, but rather than driving you into the ground over past mistakes, God prefers that you change your attitude and lifestyle. Such a change is called repentance. *"In the past God overlooked such ignorance, but now he commands all people everywhere to repent"* (Acts 17:30).

Will Jesus forgive your stewardship failures? Yes! As you answer, remember that He came to bring abundant life, to restore and make whole, to save and build up. He's much more interested in seeing the nations come to a saving knowledge of Him than harping on your past mistakes.

Get on with it. A broken and dying world desperately must hear the message of Jesus, and you're a strategic part of His plan.

Interactive — Week 1, Day 5

Do you have a difficult time believing that Jesus will forgive you for your stewardship failures?

❏ Yes   ❏ No

What specific wrong choices have come to mind this week as you have studied about how you use the resources God gives you?

money management   _____

_____

time in the Word and in prayer _____

_____

time with family_____

_____

Reread 1 John 1:9 in the Devotional. Underline the word in that verse that says how much unrighteousness you are forgiven for, if you confess.

The word *all* is critical. Sometimes you may tend to think part of your sins are forgiven but that some "biggies" exist that God could never wipe away. Some of those "biggies" may include those wrong choices you just listed. God doesn't put hierarchies on sin. Sin is sin to Him, and He forgives *all* that you confess.

Try to memorize 1 John 1:9, and then say it from memory to your spouse or to another family member or friend. Below describe a specific time in which you have experienced the joy of forgiveness for some wrongdoing in your life.

_____

_____

_____

_____

The Devotional you just read states that "God prefers that you change your attitude and lifestyle" instead of dwelling on your past wrongs.

Interactive — Week 1, Day 5

After you repent of past wrongs made, what kind of changes do you need to make? Below list one thing in each area we've studied that you commit to do to be a better steward.

money management _____

_____

time in the Word and in prayer _____

_____

time with family _____

_____

How will making choices in these three areas impact your ability to share the good news about Jesus?

money management _____

_____

time in the Word and in prayer_____

_____

time with family_____

_____

You might have answered in a manner similar to this: *If I'm not a slave to debt, I can give more money to missions or fund mission trips. If I spend more time reading my Bible, I'll be better prepared with Scripture verses to use to witness. If relationships are right at home, our family members can work together to share the gospel to people around us.*

Enlist a prayer partner. Tell that person about the stewardship commitments you've described here. Ask your prayer partner to pray that God will help you keep these commitments.

Devotional
Week 1, Day 6

Memory Verse

"May the God of hope fill you with all joy and peace as you trust in him, so that you may overflow with hope by the power of the Holy Spirit."

-Romans 15:13

In Christ, I Have Hope.

"May the God of hope fill you with all joy and peace as you trust in him, so that you may overflow with hope by the power of the Holy Spirit."

(Romans 15:13)

"I sure *hope* it doesn't rain today." Or, "I *hope* that letter arrives in today's mail." We use the word *hope* in the English language to express wishful thinking. It leaves plenty of room for doubt and uncertainty. In contrast, the biblical writers used *hope* to express a calm assurance and trust. When the apostle Paul stated, *"We have put our hope in the living God"* (1 Timothy 4:10), he wasn't wishful in his thinking. He was certain of God's salvation in Jesus Christ.

One of the chief benefits of being a Christian is having access to God's resources, including hope. Hope is much more than positive thinking or believing that your future will be smooth as silk. The saints referred to in Hebrews 11:32-40 were able to endure much suffering — not because everything worked out well for them, but because they were so deeply rooted in hope. Even if allegiance to Christ cost them their lives, they knew God's causes would ultimately triumph. That's biblical hope!

The Romans 15:13 passage yields a number of insights into biblical hope. First, God is the source of all hope. If you want genuine hope, it can be found only in God. Where He is, and when He is involved, *anything* can happen. The Bible records one instance after another of God's miraculous intervention in "hopeless" situations.

It's also interesting to note that joy and peace accompany hope in the lives of believers. Confident of God's ultimate victory, we are able to relax, know that the "battle" is over, and rest in the knowledge that Christ is Lord. Joy and peace prosper in that atmosphere.

Week 1
Day 6

Devotional *continued...*

Finally, when God fills us with hope, it overflows! When I think of things that overflow, rivers come to mind. Where does water go when it overflows the riverbanks? It naturally flows to the deepest, most low-lying locations, and there it begins to build. God desires for us to overflow with hope so that we can touch the lives of people around us who are desperately low in hope and outlook in life. Who in your realm of influence needs the hope you have found in Christ? *"For we are to God the aroma of Christ among those who are being saved and those who are perishing"* (2 Corinthians 2:15).

Living out His hope is a form of stewardship. God's plan is to fill your life to overflowing so that others who are lost — literally lost in life — can find the same hope in God. Following Christ's example, we are called to pour ourselves into the lives of others, thus building hope where there is none.

But you can't give away something you don't have. That's why your identity in Jesus Christ is so integral to your walk as a steward.

Devotional
Week 1, Day 7

This Week's Lessons

Day 1 : What is the source of my identity?

Day 2 : Does the time I spend in the Word reflect who I am in Christ?

Day 3 : Does the time I spend in prayer reflect who I am in Christ?

Day 4 : How does the time I spend with my family reflect who I am in Christ?

Day 5 : Will Jesus forgive my stewardship failures?

Day 6 : In Christ, I have hope.

Day 7 : My identity in Christ is a reason to celebrate!

Memory Verse

"I give them eternal life, and they shall never perish; no one can snatch them out of my hand."

-John 10:28

My Identity in Christ Is a Reason to Celebrate!

"I give them eternal life, and they shall never perish; no one can snatch them out of my hand." (John 10:28)

"We're number one! We're number one!" From the World Series to college football and all the way to Little League champions, all competitors strive for the top spot. There's a certain celebrity status or identity associated with being the best. It's usually marked by city-wide rallies, parades, or banquets. When we excel, achieve, and reach the top, it's wonderful to have others celebrate with us!

Unlike the temporary identity or glory of earthly champions, Jesus Christ offers permanent identity and glory as children of God. Once you're born as a child of God, you cannot be unborn. *"No one can snatch them out of my hand,"* He said. Since the life He gives is eternal, it has no end! Unlike earthly championships, the celebrations never end!

As Christians, we celebrate divine holiness and righteousness in character — an impossible feat to accomplish on our own. Though it is not natural, God transforms us with the ability to love our enemies and forgive those who have wronged us — even deliberately! Because of Christ's victory over death, the sting of death is thwarted by knowing we'll see our loved ones in Christ again in heaven. Finally, we celebrate the meaning and purpose Jesus brings to our lives here on earth. As the apostle Paul put it, *"He died for all, that those who live should no longer live for themselves but for him who died for them and was raised again"* (2 Corinthians 5:15). These are gifts from God that no one can snatch from you! They're gifts worth celebrating, aren't they?

Devotional *continued...*

There's something about joy that makes us reach out to others to make the celebration complete, and God knows that. That's why He calls us to Himself, not just as individuals but as an entire community of faith called the church. The joy and festivities of victory over sin and death are meant to be celebrated together weekly in the worship life of your church.

Despite this fact, you may have days, weeks, or even seasons of life when it is really difficult to feel the joy of belonging to Christ. But that's when you need your brothers and sisters in Christ all the more! In turn, there will be other times when God's love and grace are distinctly real, permeating the core of your soul. Perhaps that describes exactly what you're experiencing today; so, when you attend church today, be sure to seek out others who may need your encouragement. Think of attending church as an opportunity for you to give, rather than to receive. Amazingly, as you give, God will bless you, and you will receive!

Celebrations are meant to be shared. Don't let this Lord's Day pass with you missing out on the action. Sing with gusto. Pray with fervor. Listen to the proclamation of God's Word with concentration. Above all, rejoice in your identity in Christ!

Devotional
Week 2, Day 1

Memory Verse

"For where your treasure is, there your heart will be also."

-Matthew 6:21

Do My Financial Expenditures Reflect Biblical Priorities?

"For where your treasure is, there your heart will be also." (Matthew 6:21)

Before you can answer this question, you must (1) have a grasp of biblical priorities of managing money and (2) an accurate knowledge of how your money is being spent. A priority suggests that some choices are more important than others.

If you were spending money perfectly, according to God's will, what would your expenditures look like? Actually, God's Word permits great liberty in spending, governed by a few wise guidelines. God supplies resources to meet our needs (Philippians 4:19) and the needs of others (2 Corinthians 8:14-15). If you borrow, God also expects you to faithfully pay back (Ecclesiastes 5:4-5). Further, His counsel is for you to avoid signing surety — either cosigning for another person or borrowing without a sure way to repay (Proverbs 6:1-5). Finally, in all things — not just the tithe — God calls us to glorify Him. His will is for all our financial dealings to be righteous and honest. God also delights when our resources meet His overall purposes for mankind, particularly *"to seek and to save what was lost"* (Luke 19:10).

Don't make the mistake of saying to yourself, "When we get caught up financially, or when we make a certain income, then we will fully commit to handling our finances God's way." The truth is, if you don't commit to biblical priorities with what you already have, it's unlikely that you will commit when you have more money. Your heart attitude toward God, and not the amount of money, is the key issue.

Week 2
Day 1

Devotional *continued...*

The second area you must have a grasp of is your current expenditures. *"Be sure you know the condition of your flocks, give careful attention to your herds"* (Proverbs 27:23). Solomon's admonition was to pay careful attention to your measures of income. In those days it was herds of animals; today it is your bank account.

To prevent overspending, you must have a plan to ensure that all your financial obligations are met. Everyone has a spending plan of some sort, even it is disorganized. An *organized* plan is called a budget. If you're not living on a budget, your finances will likely dictate decisions for you, rather than you managing your finances under the lordship of Jesus Christ. The absence of an organized plan inevitably leads to a lack of money for surprise expenses, and it's a downhill slide from there into credit card debt.

Being a faithful steward of your finances requires that your checkbook and Bible go hand-in-hand. Jesus said, *"Do not store up for yourselves treasures on earth, where moth and rust destroy, and where thieves break in and steal. But store up for yourselves treasures in heaven . . . . For where your treasure is, there your heart will be also"* (Matthew 6:19-21). Based on your pattern of money management, would God conclude that your financial expenditures reflect biblical priorities?

Interactive — Week 2, Day 1

Every day you live, you are in the process of setting priorities. As your Devotional stated, a *priority* means that some choices are more important than others.

What are some of your current priorities? What things are most important to you at this particular time in your life? (ex.: setting aside time each day for physical exercise, eating healthy foods, establishing a regular "date night" with my spouse, etc.) Below, list several of them.

_____

_____

_____

Were you surprised when you read in the Devotional that God's Word permits great liberty in spending?

❑ Yes   ❑ No

Read Matthew 19:16-23. Why did Jesus issue to the rich young man the challenge about giving?

_____

_____

Many people have a false notion that the Bible mandates giving everything to the church, but Matthew 19, as well as the Scripture passages in the Devotional, clearly illustrates otherwise. Even in the biblical story of the rich young man, Jesus addressed a *lordship* issue that was particular to the man's case. Scripture does not demand that each person give all that he or she has to the poor. This young man was challenged to an act that would show his own particular devotion to Christ.

Have you ever made the statement that the third paragraph mentions — "When we get caught up financially, we will fully commit to handling our finances God's way?"

❑ Yes   ❑ No

If you answered yes, fill in the blanks below as you may have used these statements to apply to your financial situation.

When _____ occurs, then I will _____ _____ .

When I'm _____ , then I will _____ for the Lord.

Interactive — Week 2, Day 1

Do you have a strategic, organized plan for spending? If so, describe some characteristics of it:

_____

_____

If not, list some of the reasons why:

_____

_____

If you were to hand your checkbook to God for a line-by-line review, what would your spending indicate your top priorities are?

_____

_____

How pleased do you think God is with what your spending shows about your top priorities?

_____

_____

You may believe you manage some aspects of your finances better than other aspects. For example, you may believe that you do well with keeping your clothing and grocery expenses within bounds while your entertainment expenses are off the charts. List some ways you have chosen to manage your expenses. (Examples: using cash only for weekly expenses, cutting dining-out expenses in half, family housecleaning instead of hiring a maid service, etc.)

Below, list three areas in which you believe you manage well financially and three in which you believe chaos reigns, or at least some improvement is needed.

Doing OK	Chaos; Needs Improvement
(1)_____	(1)_____
(2)_____	(2)_____
(3)_____	(3)_____

The last paragraph of the Devotional posed the question, "Do your checkbook and Bible go hand in hand?" If you were unable to answer yes, search your heart about this. Go for a walk in your neighborhood, take a drive in the country, or find a quiet place in your home where you can meditate. During this brief retreat, ask God what mid-course correction He would have you make about aligning your spending with His Word.

Devotional
Week 2, Day 2

Memory Verse

"Yet the news about him spread all the more, so that crowds of people came to hear him and to be healed of their sicknesses. But Jesus often withdrew to lonely places and prayed".

-Luke 5:15-16

Does the Use of My Time Reflect Biblical Priorities?

"Yet the news about him spread all the more, so that crowds of people came to hear him and to be healed of their sicknesses. But Jesus often withdrew to lonely places and prayed." (Luke 5:15-16)

Periodic speaking engagements provide me the opportunity to share with people just like you and to answer questions about money management. I find that fatigue requires me to stop and return to my lodging for rest.

Yet I only have a glimpse of what Jesus must have encountered everywhere He went. Human needs were overwhelming. Going to Galilee meant He couldn't minister to the needs in Bethany, and so on. All the while, He was faced with the challenge of training the twelve disciples to carry on following His crucifixion, resurrection, and ascension into heaven. I believe the two factors that governed His time management will help you make strategic decisions about yours.

Jesus clearly understood His purpose in life. *"My food,"* said Jesus, *"is to do the will of him who sent me and to finish his work"* (John 4:34). Because of His intimate fellowship with the Father, Jesus could distinguish the activities that were essential and those that weren't (note the Luke passage above). Jesus occasionally turned away from spiritually hungry followers to be alone with the Father.

Are you clear as to why God keeps you here on the earth? What would happen if you curtailed your busyness to spend more intimate time with the Father in the Word and prayer? That's what Jesus did.

Week 2
Day 2

Devotional *continued...*

A second factor that helped Jesus successfully manage His time was being proactive about meeting the needs of others, not *reacting* to them. Knowledge of His Father's will enabled Him to remain in control. For instance, when He received the news that His friend Lazurus was at the point of death (John 11:4-6), He intentionally delayed His trip to Bethany. It wasn't that He lacked compassion; rather, He understood the big picture of how this incident could work to the Father's glory. The Father's priorities determined where and when He ministered, rather than the endless needs of people around Him.

You are likely faced with endless requests for your time at work, as a spouse, parent, church member, and citizen in your community. Saying "yes" with integrity to some commitments will necessarily mean saying "no" to others. Saying "no" enables you to concentrate on the essential matters God wants you to deal with.

Finally, here are some tips to manage your time successfully.

- Make time to plan your day, week, month, and year.

- Make your needs clearly known. Are you overwhelmed? If no one knows, how can anyone possibly help?

- Keep an accurate calendar. If you have a busy family, assign each person a color and color-code events.

- Delegate. If someone else can do it, assign it. If there's no one to delegate to, train someone.

- Allow extra time for the unexpected.

- Be prepared to sacrifice "good" activities for the sake of maintaining serenity.

Interactive — Week 2, Day 2

What things keep you from accomplishing all you have planned to do? (Check all that apply.)

- ❑ fatigue
- ❑ failure to plan
- ❑ believing that I must meet others' expectations
- ❑ unexpected time demands
- ❑ need for quantity of activities rather than quality
- ❑ other _____

What kind of measuring stick do you use to distinguish essential versus nonessential activities?

_____

_____

_____

You might have answered that you ask yourself whether the activity can wait another day without difficulty or whether it helps to further God's Kingdom. Regardless of what set of criteria you use, it's important that you set priorities strategically rather than being swept along by a tide of purposeless busyness. Sometimes we must choose among "good," better" and "best."

Have you ever said "no" to activities that seemed pressing in order to spend time alone with the Father?

❑ Yes   ❑ No

If so, what did you do to make room in your schedule for God?

_____

_____

_____

You might have answered that you set the alarm early to get up for a quiet time, turned off the TV before the evening news, or set aside a noontime shopping trip or a coffee break at work to devote some time to Bible study.

Taking such steps requires courage, but you'll experience heavenly dividends as a result.

Interactive — Week 2, Day 2

What is your purpose in life? As you read your Day 2 material, how did you answer the question, "Are you clear as to why God keeps you here on earth?"

_____

_____

_____

Study how your expenditures of time mesh with your life purpose. Ask yourself whether your tasks help you further your purpose here on earth or whether they detract from it. This may help you gauge how you spend the moments of your day.

Why is saying "no" to people's requests of you a difficult thing to do?

- ❑ I have a difficult time knowing what my priorities should be.
- ❑ I'm afraid people won't like me if I turn them down.
- ❑ It's difficult for me to be direct with people.
- ❑ I'm so unsure of myself, it's difficult for me to know what I want.
- ❑ I'm afraid they'll never ask me again.
- ❑ Saying "no" might damage my image as a do-gooder.
- ❑ Other _____

Can you think of a Scripture passage that helps you say "no" when it's appropriate to do so? For example, some that might come to mind are Galatians 1:10, Proverbs 16:3, and Proverbs 3:5-6. Which ones help you?

_____

_____

_____

Reread the list of tips at the end of the Devotional. Put one star by the suggestion that's easiest for you to do and two stars by the one that's most difficult for you. Then below, write a one-sentence prayer asking God to help you accomplish the suggestion you think will be toughest to follow.

_____

_____

_____

Week 2, Day 3

Memory Verse

"A prudent man sees danger and takes refuge, but the simple keep going and suffer for it."

-Proverbs 22:3

How Do My Financial Goals Affect My Family?

"A prudent man sees danger and takes refuge, but the simple keep going and suffer for it." (Proverbs 22:3)

Setting financial goals can be a challenge for committed Christians. On the one hand, some see goal-setting as the antithesis of faith. Since God will provide anyway, there's no need for goals, they assert. Others set rigid goals, refuse to modify them, and reduce money management to a series of formulas and calculations, with faith and flexibility eliminated. The wise approach strikes a balance between these two extremes.

Setting financial goals can become an exciting statement of faith. A goal of any sort simply states an aspiration, desired outcome, or objective. The apostle Paul's letters are replete with goal statements, such as: *"I want to know Christ and the power of his resurrection and the fellowship of sharing in his sufferings . . ."* (Philippians 3:10).

Financial goals not only define your objectives for the future, such as one year, three years, five years, and so on, but the goals often offer guidance to the plans you will (and won't) use to get you there. For instance, you may have a goal of being debt free in five years. Another goal you may set is always to be honest in all of your financial dealings, including your income tax returns. Thus, goals define ultimate outcomes as well as the behaviors or plans to take you to those outcomes.

You probably can see how your family life will be impacted by the goals you set and maintain. If your goal is to be debt free in five years, you may decide to repair and continue driving your old "clunker" car another year or two, rather than leasing a brand new vehicle. Overall, you likely will live a more frugal lifestyle if you set the goal of being debt free in the

Devotional *continued...*

future. By prayerfully setting financial goals, you set a precedent for your children to follow as they grow up, leave home, and establish their own families.

Goals are not carved in stone; they can and should be modified as circumstances warrant. For that reason, setting and maintaining financial goals require intimate fellowship with God and a thorough knowledge of His Word. After all, you wouldn't want to set goals contrary to the principles in His written Word.

The risk of *not* setting goals is constantly facing one financial emergency after another. *"A prudent man sees danger and takes refuge, but the simple keep going and suffer for it"* (Proverbs 22:3). The chaos created by that lifestyle can have a damaging impact on your family. Often one spouse or both take a second or third job to recover from indebtedness caused by — you guessed it — a lack of clear financial goals.

Are your financial goals clear? If not, why not? Goal-setting can enhance unity in your marriage, shape current spending patterns, and engender hope by providing direction for the future. Start today by detailing where you believe God wants you to be financially one year from now!

Interactive — Week 2, Day 3

The Devotional listed two perspectives that people have on setting financial goals. Which of the two perspectives on setting financial goals do you follow? Below, mark a spot on the line between the two perspectives that would indicate where you fall.

_____

God Provides   *Rigid Plan*
No Need for   *No Faith*
* Goals*   *Required*

Below, recall times in which you have set specific financial goals in the past. How far did you go in accomplishing these goals?

Goal   Outcome

_____

_____

_____

Sometimes it helps to examine which of your past goals were truly practical and attainable and which ones were "blue-sky," or impossible to achieve.

Go back to the goals you listed above. Write a "P" by the ones you now realize were practical and attainable and a "B" by the ones which were "blue-sky," or impossible to achieve.

The goal of this Devotional is to help you study the impact on your family when you have financial goals versus the impact on your family when you fail to set them.

Can you look back on how your family responded during times when you were without specific financial goals? (Ex.: We had no budget, so I spent lots of money on toys for the children. The kids were not appreciative, so I yelled at them, but I was actually angry at myself for my own excesses. Or, I criticized my wife for spending too much on clothing, but I later realized that I had failed to set a clothing budget for her to follow. My criticism of her was hurtful to her.)

Interactive — Week 2, Day 3

Below, describe similar incidents in which your family was impacted by lack of financial goals.

_____

_____

_____

Has your family ever been in chaos because it faced one financial emergency after another? If so, describe below.

_____

_____

_____

The Devotional names one blessing — positive role-modeling for children — that can occur when parents are frugal and manage well. Describe some blessings you have experienced during a period of frugality.

_____

_____

_____

The Devotional mentions Proverbs 22:3 as an instruction from God's Word that can help you in setting goals. What are some other Scripture verses that you have relied on to help you set financial goals? List them here.

_____

_____

_____

Do as the Devotional suggests. Start detailing where you believe God wants you to be financially a year from now. Conduct a family council. You can do this even if you are married with no children in the home. If you are single, set aside some special time for goal-setting.

To conduct a family council, agree on a meeting time and place. Post an agenda and ask for topic suggestions. Begin with prayer. Establish rules for brainstorming. Issues could include everything from allowances to how to save for a family vacation to how to reduce spending in a certain area. Set a date for a follow-up meeting.

Week 2, Day 4

Memory Verse

"As each one has received a special gift, employ it in serving one another, as good stewards of the manifold grace of God."

-1 Peter 4:10 NASB

Have I Made a Priority of Exercising My Spiritual Gifts?

"As each one has received a special gift, employ it in serving one another, as good stewards of the manifold grace of God." (1 Peter 4:10 NASB)

Don't fall into the mentality of going to church to get a blessing. That thinking sets you up to critique the sermon, the choir's performance, the soloist, the accompanist, the Sunday School lesson, and the teacher. Your attitude will remain self-centered and focused on what others can do for you. In contrast, God desires for you to attend church to give — in worship and in service to others. It's a paradox: The more you give, the more you receive.

Peter's admonition is a sobering reminder that God intends for you to use your spiritual gifts. God's plan for you extends beyond just saving you; His desire is to work through you to touch the lives of others. Accordingly, your spiritual gifts must be used to minister to others. As you use them, the church family is strengthened. The apostle Paul confirmed this very insight when he wrote, *"From him the whole body, joined and held together by every supporting ligament, grows and builds itself up in love, as each part does its work"* (Ephesians 4:16).

Can you identify your spiritual gifts? If you can't, why not obtain and complete a copy of *Ministry Gifts Inventory*?[1] Knowing your gifts will clarify the role God desires for you to fulfill in your church. After all, how well would a professional baseball team fare if the catcher played right field, the left fielder became the pitcher, and the shortstop played the catcher position? Failing to determine and use your spiritual gifts leaves the body of Christ equally disorganized and weakened, much like a stroke victim experiences paralysis.

Week 2

Day 4

Devotional *continued...*

Be deliberate in using your gift to serve. Many believers, for instance, have the gift of exhortation (Romans 12:8 NASB). They can listen to another person's problems and help that person to find hope in Christ for those circumstances. If you have that gift, use it daily. When you go to church, find someone to encourage, and don't leave until you have exercised your gift. The same is true with other gifts, including teaching, leading, or offering mercy (Romans 12:6-8). Someone needs what you have to offer each Lord's Day, not to mention throughout the week.

Finally, maintain a humble attitude in serving with your gifts. God's church has suffered great heartache at the hands of some who would elevate their particular gifts above the rest. The apostle Paul taught that *"The body is a unit, though it is made up of many parts . . ."* (1 Corinthians 12:12). You are not the entire body, and neither should you minimize the gifts of others (1 Corinthians 12:21-27). A humble attitude recognizes the contributions that others with different gifts make to church life.

With regard to spiritual gifts, would you say you are a spectator or a servant? Do you go to church more to *get* or to *give?* The secret of getting blessed is first being a blessing to God and to others!

[1] Michael Miller, *Ministry Gifts Inventory* (Nashville: Convention Press, 1995)

Interactive , Week 2, Day 4

Are you guilty of the attitude that paragraph 1 of the Devotional describes — going to church to get instead of to give? Have you ever been a spectator and not a participant?

❑ Yes   ❑ No

Perhaps this Devotional piqued your conscience about a time in which you had a critical spirit about church leaders as you participated in a worship service or church activity. If so, stop and confess this to God. Ask Him to forgive you and show you what you might do to help build up instead of tear down these individuals. Below, write one step you could take to be part of a solution at your church instead of being part of the problem by criticizing.

_____

_____

_____

Can you give a testimony about a time in which the more you gave of your time and abilities in a church situation, the more you received? If so, describe that time here. (Example: I volunteered to lead a Bible study for homeless persons. The determined attitudes of many encouraged me during a "down" time in my life.)

_____

_____

_____

Using your spiritual gifts that God gave you is not an option; it's a command of God. How do you feel when you're reminded of this? (Check any of the statements below that apply to your attitude.)

❑ Why would anyone want my contribution? I have nothing to offer.
❑ I'm just one of many people with this gift. I'm sure others can do it better.
❑ Maybe I'm gifted, but I simply don't have time to serve.
❑ I'm not sure what my gift is, but I want to identify it.
❑ I'm afraid if I use my gift, I'll do it wrong or people will ridicule me.
❑ I want to be obedient and use my gift as God leads.
❑ Other _____

Interactive, Week 2, Day 4

Describe a time in which you believe you used your spiritual gifts as God commanded. How do you believe the use of them strengthened the body?

_____

_____

_____

Reread the first sentence of paragraph 2 in the Devotional. How has God worked through you to touch another person's life in the past week? Describe one experience you can recall.

_____

_____

_____

Locate a spiritual-gifts inventory, such as the one the Devotional mentions or another one.[1] Take the inventory, if you have not already taken one. Then find a trusted person, such as a Sunday School teacher, accountability partner, church-staff member, discipleship-group leader, or another mature Christian. Ask that person to help you process the outcome of your spiritual-gifts inventory. Ask that person to help you identify your spiritual gifts and ways you can use them to support the church body. Below, write a paragraph describing the outcome of your conversation.

_____

_____

_____

_____

_____

_____

(See Plan of Salvation on next page.)

[1] Michael Miller, *Ministry Gifts Inventory* (Nashville: Convention Press, 1995)

PLAN OF SALVATION

CLAIMING YOUR INHERITANCE

Lauren is having an identity crisis. It isn't the first time and she's sure it won't be the last. With every new season of life, with each new crisis, she is overcome with self-doubt, self-blame and a deep feeling of insecurity.

"Who is the real me," she wonders, *"and would I like her if I knew?"*

Fortunately, there is good news for Lauren — and for you, as well. You see, Lauren is loved deeply and unconditionally by one who knows her inside and out. And so are you. He knows your every mistake, every selfish thought, every untrue action. He knows and loves you anyway.

God is the lover of Lauren's soul — and yours. He created you in loving kindness. He gave you wonderful gifts to be discovered, priceless pearls designed for you to use to make a difference in the world. He has an incredible inheritance for you. All you have to do is claim it.

By becoming a member of God's family, Lauren can receive her inheritance from Him. And so can you. How is this possible?

The Bible tells us that we all fall short of God's righteous standard. Because of this, we are separated from Him and spiritually dead (Romans 3:23). But because God loves us, He provided a way for us to connect with Him and to be empowered by Him. John 3:16 says "For God so loved the world that he gave his one and only Son, that whoever believes in him shall not perish but have eternal life." God sent Jesus, who lived a perfect life, to die on the cross as a payment for our sin.

By accepting the gift of His son Jesus, we can establish a love relationship with God — one that is personal and permanent. Even death cannot sever it.

YOU can begin a love relationship with God right now and claim YOUR royal inheritance as a son or daughter of the King of Kings. If you are ready to make this choice, as an affirmation of your belief, simply pray a prayer something like this: Dear God, I understand I am a sinner. But I believe Jesus died to pay for my sins and I now accept His gift of eternal life. Thank you for forgiving my sins. Thank you for my new life. From this day on, I choose to follow You and Your will for my life.

If you decided to begin a love relationship with God through His son Jesus, please share this decision with a Christian friend, a pastor or someone in your church right away!

Devotional
Week 2, Day 5

Memory Verse

"For we must all appear before the judgment seat of Christ, that each one may receive what is due him for the things done in the body, whether good or bad."

-2 Corinthians 5:10

Am I Accountable for Establishing and Maintaining My Priorities?

"For we must all appear before the judgment seat of Christ, that each one may receive what is due him for the things done in the body, whether good or bad."

(2 Corinthians 5:10)

One day you will stand face-to-face with Jesus Christ. Eye-to-eye. Not with your church family. Not with your parents, your spouse, or your pastor. *"Each one"* is what the Word of God says. Just you and Jesus. It will be an awesome moment.

The purpose of the meeting will not be to determine your salvation. You should have complete assurance that you are heaven-bound in the instant following your last breath here on earth (John 5:24). Only unbelievers will appear before the Great White Throne judgment referenced in Revelation 20:11-15, the last stop prior to their departure into an eternity of torment.

The judgment seat of Christ is completely different, however, since it will be a joyous celebration of the godly victories in your life. Your mind may struggle to comprehend it, but it may be like a supernatural video replay of your life. With Jesus, you'll celebrate the times when you were tempted, that God provided a way of escape (1 Corinthians 10:13), and your love for Jesus was greater than the allurement of sin. Perhaps you'll be pleasantly surprised at godly, caring deeds you had done in Jesus' name, like the righteous servants described in Matthew 25:37-39. They fed the hungry, offered drink to the thirsty, provided clothing to the poor, offered hospitality to strangers, and visited the sick and prisoners. In short, they invested their lives in expressing God's love to the needy and disenfranchised. How are you serving Christ in your life?

Week 2
Day 5

Devotional *continued...*

In the meantime, God's plan is for you to be accountable here on earth. Fellow Christians can help you to faithfully serve Jesus if you will allow them. *"As iron sharpens iron, so one man sharpens another"* (Proverbs 27:17). Some find accountability with their pastor or Sunday School teacher. Others hold each other accountable in home Bible studies or prayer clusters of three or four people.

But what about you? Is there anyone who really knows what's happening in your life — the burdens you carry, the temptations you face, and the victories you experience? *"Two are better than one, because they have a good return for their work: If one falls down, his friend can help him up. But pity the man who falls and has no one to help him up!"* (Ecclesiastes 4:9-10). Everyone should have someone. Becoming accountable here on earth will help you to be prepared for your ultimate accountability meeting with God! And what a pity it would be if you lived your life without anyone really knowing you!

Are you ready to stand before Jesus Christ at His judgment seat? If not, what changes do you need to make in your life today? Will you trust someone enough to hold you accountable for those changes?

Interactive — Week 2, Day 5

Have you ever believed that you could hide behind the good deeds or accomplishments of another person?

❑ Yes   ❑ No

Most people, if they're honest, can admit to times they believed, or wished, they could get to heaven on someone else's coattails. Many people have heard the expression, "God doesn't have any grandchildren." You are responsible for your own salvation. Just because your father or your sister or husband is a Christian doesn't mean you can inherit eternal life. Your salvation requires a personal encounter with Jesus Christ. So does your living out the Christian life. As your Devotional mentions, no one else can do this for you.

What will be shown on the big-screen replay of your life when you're face to face with Jesus Christ?

Can you describe a time —

. . . when God provided you a way of escape from temptation?

_____

_____

. . . when you performed a caring deed in Jesus' name?

_____

_____

. . . when you witnessed for Christ?

_____

_____

. . . when you visited the sick, hungry, or disenfranchised?

_____

_____

Describe a time in which you've experienced "iron sharpening iron" (Prov. 27:17) as you have interacted —

. . . with another individual Christian.

_____

_____

. . . with a group of people, such as a support group, prayer group, or Bible study group.

_____

_____

You might have mentioned a time in which you've explored the meaning of a Bible passage with a friend or when someone has, in love, reminded you that you were straying from a Christlike way. Stop and say a silent prayer of thanks to God for putting these individuals or groups in your path.

Your Devotional's fifth paragraph mentions the need for someone to know what's really happening in your life. What person or persons came to mind as you read this? In the roles listed below, jot down the initials of the person you thought about. (One person may fill all these roles, or you may name a variety of individuals.)

Who knows—
    . . . the burdens you carry? _____
    . . . the temptations you face? _____
    . . . the victories you experience? _____

Who holds you accountable for your financial stewardship?

_____

_____

If you don't have the initials of people listed in some or all of these categories above, stop and pray about whom God would have you select.

Is trust an issue as you think about finding someone to hold you accountable? Maybe you have a difficult time with trust because significant people in your life, such as parents, were not trustworthy in the past. God can help you overcome your hesitation in this area. Maybe you need to make this concern a part of your prayer. If you do have accountability people in your life, stop and thank God for these individuals to whom you can relate in these specific areas.

Devotional
Week 2, Day 6

Memory Verse

"The plans of the dili-
gent lead to profit as
surely as haste leads to
poverty."

-Proverbs 21:5

Will My Priorities Lead to Financial Freedom?

"The plans of the diligent lead to profit as surely as haste leads to poverty."
(Proverbs 21:5)

Are your patterns of money management leading to financial freedom or to bondage? To answer, you must first have a clear picture of what financial freedom really is.

Financial freedom includes an absence of worries over money, overdue bills, threats from collection agencies, or the panic of never having enough money. Beyond the actual handling of money, financial freedom also penetrates the spiritual dimensions of your life, bringing freedom from envy, greed, and jealousy. Jesus noted, *"The pagans run after all these things"* (Matthew 6:32), and His Word calls us to live distinctly differently than pagans (Colossians 3:2; 1 Peter 2:11-12).

But financial freedom also describes the liberty to live out God's will for our lives. Financial freedom results from committing all aspects of life to God and by faithfully obeying His principles. It's not determined by huge sums of money laid in store. You may have no debt, hundreds of thousands of dollars in the bank, and still be in financial bondage. On the other hand, you may be financially free with only a modest amount of your income saved in reserve.

As a financially free person, you are available to respond to the promptings of the Holy Spirit. When God shows you someone's needs, you will have financial resources to help meet those needs. You can see how financial freedom enables you to fulfill God's plan for your life.

Week 2
Day 6

Devotional *continued...*

A plan leading to financial freedom begins by transferring ownership of everything to God, including debts and financial mistakes. If Jesus forgives your spiritual sins, He will certainly forgive your financial mistakes and help you to proceed with the plan He has for your life. In faith, commit all your ways and resources to Him.

The next step toward financial freedom involves eliminating all debt. Be aware that this may take several years to accomplish. To accelerate debt reduction, you may either increase your income, decrease your spending, or both. The danger of simply increasing your income is that most people just find new ways to spend the extra money. The most effective ways of becoming debt free include some measure of cutting back expenses, such as selling an automobile, eating out less, foregoing vacations, or perhaps even selling a home. If you are saying to yourself, "Those are big changes," you're right. Becoming financially free is not a quick fix to deliver you from financial pressures. It's a lifestyle of total commitment to living for God!

So, back to the initial question. Are your patterns of money management leading to financial freedom or bondage? Will your current spending patterns lead to becoming debt free or being deeper in debt? Are you able to consistently save? When the Holy Spirit prompts you to meet needs, do you have financial resources available?

The truth of the matter is that you cannot be financially free without first being spiritually free. We'll talk about that tomorrow.

Devotional
Week 2, Day 7

Memory Verse

"I write these things to you who believe in the name of the Son of God so that you may know that you have eternal life."

-1 John 5:13

What in the World Are You Doing?

"I write these things to you who believe in the name of the Son of God so that you may know that you have eternal life." (1 John 5:13)

I hardly know a thing about my relatives who lived 100 years ago. If Jesus doesn't return, my relatives 100 years from now won't know very much about me. Everything here on earth is temporary. Isaiah once observed, *"The grass withers and the flowers fall, because the breath of the Lord blows on them. Surely the people are grass"* (Isaiah 40:7). The apostle James said, *"You are a mist that appears for a little while and then vanishes"* (James 4:14). Poof! And your life on earth will be over.

Two things last for eternity besides the Trinity: the Word of God (Isaiah 40:8) and human souls (Matthew 25:46). You're mistaken if you only strive for a bigger house, nicer car, and more money in the bank. God's Word declares all these material things will one day be destroyed by fire (2 Peter 3:10). The apostle Peter goes on to ask a poignant question: *"Since everything will be destroyed in this way, what kind of people ought you to be?"* (2 Peter 3:11). The apostle Paul advised Timothy, *"For we brought nothing into the world, and we can take nothing out of it"* (1 Timothy 6:7).

Have you ever stopped to take inventory of your life? What in the world are you doing, literally? Are your days nothing more than a series of coincidences, surviving the weeks to collapse on the weekends, only to turn around and do it again?

The key to life is simple: Nothing ultimately makes sense apart from Jesus Christ. Indeed, Paul summarized the reason for our existence on earth this way: *"All things were created by him and for him. He is before all things, and in him all things hold together"* (Colossians 1:16-17).

Devotional *continued...*

Do you know Him personally? Is He the reason you exist? Are you certain that you would go straight into the arms of Jesus if you died later today? I didn't ask you if you were a church member or how much money you have given to the church; I asked if you are positive you're headed for heaven. Are you?

The testimony of Scripture is that you can be certain about where you will spend eternity. *"And this is the testimony: God has given us eternal life, and this life is in his Son. He who has the Son has life; he who does not have the Son of God does not have life. I write these things to you who believe in the name of the Son of God so that you may know that you have eternal life"* (1 John 5:11-13).

If you're not positive about your relationship with Jesus, please alert your pastor, a deacon, or a mature Christian friend today. Don't delay; you may not have tomorrow. And, if you're certain of *your* salvation, who else will be in heaven because of your life and witness?

Devotional
Week 3, Day 1

Memory Verse

"For those God foreknew he also predestined to be conformed to the likeness of his Son . . . ."

-Romans 8:29

Why Should I Give?

"For those God foreknew he also predestined to be conformed to the likeness of his Son . . . ." (Romans 8:29)

It is amazing how little children mimic their parents. Getting into momma's makeup and playing with plastic hammers, saws, and lawn mowers are popular activities with little girls and boys, trying to be like mom and dad. And when the little ones do something cute, they're acting like your side of the family, but misdeeds come from your spouse's side. Right? I know how it goes.

It is even more natural for God's children to desire to be just like Him. Being saved means much more than settling your eternal destination. Salvation includes being *"conformed to the likeness of his Son,"* (Romans 8:29) which means that we begin to think, feel, and act like Jesus. Nowhere is this insight more important than in the area of giving.

God calls you to be a generous person because that's the way He is; He generously gives His grace and mercy to us in Christ. The apostle John put it like this: *"For of His fulness we have all received, and grace upon grace"* (John 1:16 NASB). With respect to your salvation, would you say that God has given you strictly what you deserve, or has He been generous in forgiving and cleansing you? Surely the latter is true, which triggers some tough questions. Are you like Him now? Do you even desire to be like Him in every regard, including being generous? Is becoming like Him the passion of your life?

Week 3
Day 1

Devotional *continued...*

Once you belong to Christ, His intent is for you to act like Him, and that necessarily includes being generous. Selfishness is not part of God's character. Instead, to foster His generous character in you, God will make the needs of other people evident so you can exhibit His love and care. Just ask God to make you a more generous spouse, parent, or neighbor, and watch how quickly God creates opportunities to share His love!

Here's the key insight: Love seeks the needs in others and finds a way to make provision for them. It's impossible to sincerely seek to discover the needs of others in your church, community, and the world, and not to be part of the solution. Indeed, the apostle John pressed with this question, *"If anyone has material possessions and sees his brother in need but has no pity on him, how can the love of God be in him?"* (1 John 3:17).

Since generosity is a way of life, it touches attitudes and relationships far beyond money management. You can be generous with time, attention, and affection. Generosity means allowing another car to cut in front of you, in spite of the traffic jam. It means seeing yourself as an endless reservoir of God's blessing and encouragement in a world that is desperately hungry for love, affirmation, and hope.

Knowing that God explicitly wills for you to be a generous person, are you cooperating with Him or resisting Him?

Interactive — Week 3, Day 1

In the second paragraph, your Day 1 Devotional study quoted Romans 8:29 to remind you that you are "conformed to the likeness of his Son" at salvation. Three other Scripture passages listed below also remind you to keep Christ as your model as well. Look up each of them in your Bible, and then answer the question below.

John 15:12   John 15:10   1 Peter 2:23

Name two specific ways in which you believe you follow Christ as your role model.

_____

_____

_____

Maybe you answered something like this: *I try to spend time with the Father as Christ did. I strive to forgive others who wrong me. I try to be a peacemaker in relationships. I constantly work on loving others.*

As a Christian, you are not without specific directions on how you are to live. The Bible gives you the particulars of how you are to think, feel, and act like Jesus.

The third paragraph asks you whether you would consider generosity the "passion of your life," as you strive to be like Christ. On the following scale of 0 *(not important at all)* to 10 *(highly important)*, put a mark indicating where you would rate yourself in this category.

```
_____
0     1     2     3     4     5     6     7     8     9     10
```

The Bible says that God gave us of "His fulness" — in other words, generously (John 1:16, NASB). You can follow in His steps.

Look around you. How is God right now making other peoples' needs evident to you, so that you might respond generously? Look at the three categories that the Devotional mentioned. Describe a need that you might meet, or be in the process of meeting, in each category.

a need my spouse has _____

_____

a need my child has _____

_____

a need my neighbor or friend has _____

_____

Have you ever resisted when God prompted you to give more generously of your money, time, attention, or affection?

❑ Yes   ❑ No

If you answered "Yes," describe below how you resisted Him in this area.

_____

_____

_____

Your answer might have been similar to these examples: *I felt God calling me to serve on a volunteer mission trip, but I told Him I was too busy. I knew He wanted me to visit a bereaved neighbor, but I spent time on my own activities. I realize I should have given the Lord more of my money last year, but I gave in to my selfish wants instead.*

The Bible reminds you in Romans 8:26 that the Spirit helps you in your weakness. If you truly desire to give more generously of your time, money, attention, and affection, but you struggle to do so, call on God to give you an extra boost in this area. Ask Him to help you do what it takes to be available to Him.

Stop and pray about the matter just mentioned.

Then, find a clean sheet of paper. Cut it into a narrow strip that will fit into your Bible. Write on it today's date and a statement, in your own words, that will remind you of your commitment to having a more giving spirit as you try to become like Him.

Devotional
Week 3, Day 2

Memory Verse

"The rich rule over the poor, and the borrower is servant to the lender."

-Proverbs 22:7

Why Can't I Give More?

"The rich rule over the poor, and the borrower is servant to the lender."

(Proverbs 22:7)

The Cat in the Hat, Garfield, Spiderman, and Bullwinkle — they're among the more popular hot air balloons treating spectators every year at the annual Macy's Thanksgiving Day parade. But 40-mph wind gusts transformed the balloons from entertainment to danger during the 1997 parade.[1] Handlers struggled to control the balloons as winds sent them hurtling toward sidewalk spectators, injuring several persons.

Debt is like those winds because it drives people into making decisions they wouldn't otherwise choose, often leaving havoc and suffering in its path. The number one cause of marriage conflict is money,[2] and credit card abuses account for 90 percent of all personal bankruptcy filings.[3] Out-of-control spending can and will wreak disaster on family life.

As you contemplated yesterday's material, perhaps you realized that you really want to be available to God, but debts prevent you. Maybe you heard about a single mother who just couldn't pay the rent, fix the car, and get her sick children to the doctor all in the same month. God may have burdened your heart to help, but you couldn't because you were overwhelmed with debt payments. Perhaps the burden was to give to your church's multicultural ministry or to send your teenager to a state conference with the youth group. You wanted to, but money was just too tight.

The Hebrews understood this predicament clearly. One of their words translating into English as "borrow" literally means to "to twine together, to unite, to abide with or cleave, or to join oneself to a lender." Another word literally means "to entangle." When you borrow, you

Week 3
Day 2

Devotional *continued...*

become obligated to the lender, who rightfully will hold you to a repayment schedule. Are you entangled with debt and money problems, rendering you unable to respond to God's prompting?

Though the Bible does not say it's a sin to borrow, doing so may leave you in a predicament like the balloon handlers — prevailing forces may prevent you from going where you really want to go! Is there anything more important in your life than being available to God, to serve Him wherever or however He prompts you?

Contrast that uncomfortable experience with the description found in Proverbs 10:22: *"It is the blessing of the Lord that makes rich, And He adds no sorrow to it"* (NASB). Worry and sorrow are not part of God's financial plan for you. When you're living at the level of lifestyle God intends for you, He will bless you with peace.

If you're not debt-free today, will you commit to a plan to take you there? People seldom get in debt overnight; neither do they get out of debt overnight. It may take a number of years. If that sounds discouraging, keep in mind that being debt-free is a lifestyle, not God's quick-fix to bail you out of a financial jam.[4] And if taking years to pay off your debts sounds too discouraging, consider the consequences of doing nothing.

[1] www.athensnewspapers.com/1997/112897/1128.a3macysparade.html (11/30/98)

[2] www.nccs.org/121096.html (3/24/98)

[3] *Money*, August 1996, page 64

[4] See "How to Get Out of Debt," pages 107-112

Interactive

Were you surprised when you read in paragraph 2 of the Devotional the statement that money is the number one cause of marriage conflict?

❑ Yes ❑ No

If you have experienced conflict in your marriage over money, check one (or more) of the statements below that describes the nature of the conflict.

❑ extent to which you call on relatives to bail you out of financial tight spots
❑ degree to which credit cards should be used for purchases
❑ disagreements over whether (and when) to make major purchases
❑ degree to which children should be responsible for their financial needs
❑ inadequate communication about financial decisions
❑ method for resolving long-term debt
❑ disagreements over long-term financial goals
❑ disagreements over spending and saving habits
❑ other _____

Have you ever wanted to help meet a need that God placed on your heart, such as those mentioned in paragraph 3, but you couldn't because of your own overwhelming debt? If so describe below.

_____
_____
_____

In John 15:13, Christ admonishes you to show others such great love that you would be willing to lay down your life for a friend. The entanglement of debt can be so pervasive that your hands are physically tied, even when you feel led to give sacrificially.

The Devotional mentions that God will bless you with peace if you are living at the level of lifestyle God intends for you. Has there ever been a time in which the Holy Spirit prompted you not to incur a debt? Perhaps you realized it was a "wish" or "desire" in excess of what your lifestyle required instead of a need. If so, describe below.

_____
_____

Read Matthew 17:20. How do you feel when you realize that you have the ability, with God's help, to set aside encompassing debt that holds you in its tentacles?

- ❑ hopeless — I've tried this before and it's not possible.
- ❑ worthless — Why should God care about my indebtedness?
- ❑ worried — What will happen to my family if I try this?
- ❑ eager — I want to trust God with this serious matter.
- ❑ other _____

I hope you were able to say that God is in charge in your life and that you are looking to Him for strength and solutions. Your Day 3 study will focus more on relying on God's power instead of your frail, human efforts.

If you truly desire the peace that comes from setting aside worry over finances, what might be the first step you would take in living a debt-free life?

_____

_____

You might have mentioned one or more of these suggestions: *conferring with a financial counselor, selling excessive possessions, finding a financial accountability partner, adapting a "cash-only" lifestyle, trimming unnecessary expenses, evaluating planned major purchases, or scaling down your residential needs.*

Stop and pray, asking God to enable you to take that first step you listed.

Devotional
Week 3, Day 3

Memory Verse

"He who did not spare his own Son, but gave him up for us all—how will he not also, along with him, graciously give us all things?"

-Romans 8:32

Do I Really Trust God to Meet My Needs?

"He who did not spare his own Son, but gave him up for us all—how will he not also, along with him, graciously give us all things?" (Romans 8:32)

Adam and Eve's fall began by doubting God's kindness. Despite the abundance of the Garden, Satan beguiled them into thinking that God was providing less than His best for their needs. Failing to trust God left them vulnerable to sinful attitudes and actions, as it will for you. Do you trust God to meet your needs?

Consider this as you ponder. The Scriptures describe God as kind (Titus 3:4, Ephesians 2:7), meaning He never wavers in desiring what's best for you. After all, He sacrificed His own Son on your behalf, so why would He not also provide for your daily needs?

Nevertheless, if you struggle to believe God will meet your needs, here are some possibilities. You may be confusing your legitimate needs with your wants and desires. The apostle Paul names food and clothing as basic needs in 1 Timothy 6:8. You may *want* to be a homeowner, and *desire* to own a home on the fashionable side of town. God promised to supply resources to meet your needs. Your responsibility, as a steward, is to live within those resources.

If you sense that your needs are being overlooked by God, another possibility is that you may be asking with the wrong motive (James 4:3). To correct your motive, deal with a character issue, or perhaps plan something even better for you, the Lord may delay in supplying your need. If His answer to your prayer is "Wait," don't mistakenly doubt His kindness. You can be assured that He wants only the best for you and your loved ones.

Week 3
Day 3

Devotional *continued...*

Finally, it could be that He has made the provision, but those resources remain under someone else's control. That's why it's important to make your needs known to your church. God provides a surplus to some so they, in turn, can give freely to those who are lacking (2 Corinthians 8:14-15). In providing this way, He creates a powerful witness to His love by the way His people love one another. Let's face it: freely giving to others is different from the selfish ways of the world.

On the other hand, if you have an abundance, your responsibility is to wisely seek God's guidance about whom you are to help. Someone is praying to God for help, and you are the answer. By generously giving, you meet the needs of others, build their confidence and faith in God, and fulfill God's purpose in supplying you the abundance.

Doubting God's kindness toward you evaporates as you consider this truth. *"Very rarely will anyone die for a righteous man, though for a good man someone might possibly dare to die. But God demonstrates his own love for us in this: While we were still sinners, Christ died for us"* (Romans 5:7-8). Will you now trust Him to meet your needs?

Interactive — Week 3, Day 3

Do you know a person you would describe as genuinely kind? In the spaces below, jot down that person's initials. Then briefly describe why the person fits that description.

_____

_____

Some possible responses might be: *the individual performs thoughtful gestures, puts my needs needs before his or her own, or acts respectfully toward me, whether or not I deserve it.*

If this particular individual epitomizes kindness to you, think how much more wonderfully kind is your perfect Heavenly Father. Perhaps this visualization may help you as you consider just how much God desires to bless you and provide for you.

Have you ever asked for something with the wrong motive? Below are some possible motives that can lie behind your requests of God. Put a check by any that you have experienced. Then describe something you learned when your motives were not pure.

- ❏ to impress my neighbors
- ❏ to cover up for some emotional hurt
- ❏ to make me feel worthy
- ❏ to achieve a certain social standing
- ❏ other _____

From the experience of asking with the wrong motives, I learned:

_____

_____

Describe a time when you received a "wait" answer from God.

_____

_____

Looking back on the situation, what can you see that God was trying to teach you through the delay? _____

_____

Interactive — Week 3, Day 3

If you are experiencing a need, to whom have you made that need known *(Example: your church, a benevolent friend or relative, a charitable agency, a generous neighbor)?*

_____

_____

_____

Are there perhaps other persons or institutions to whom you should speak about your need? Below, creatively brainstorm a little. Jot down any ideas that pop into your head, even if they might seem silly or far-fetched. Write the initials of persons or places where you might still consider making an appeal.

_____

_____

_____

That person might be blessed with an abundance that he or she is eager to use for God's purposes! You may enable that person to share his or her blessing.

If you are one of those persons blessed with an abundance, where might you look for some people to bless? Write the initials of people to whom God might lead you to give.

_____

_____

_____

In the last paragraph of your Devotional, read the Scripture listed there (Romans 5:7-8), and underline the great gift that God made available for you.

From the foundation of the world, God knew your need for a Savior and responded by sending His Son. All your other needs pale in comparison to your need for salvation.

Stop and thank Him for Jesus, the ultimate gift. Then think of someone with whom you need to share that good news.

Devotional
Week 3, Day 4

Memory Verse

"You have planted much, but have harvested little. You eat, but never have enough. You drink, but never have your fill. You put on clothes, but are not warm. You earn wages, only to put them in a purse with holes in it."

-Haggai 1:6

What If I Choose Not to Give?

"You have planted much, but have harvested little. You eat, but never have enough. You drink, but never have your fill. You put on clothes, but are not warm. You earn wages, only to put them in a purse with holes in it."

(Haggai 1:6)

Did you ever play a game called "King of the Hill" as a child? The goal was to stand at the top of a hillside and simply push aggressors back down the hill. The person remaining at the top of the hill the longest was crowned king.

Money management may seem like that game to you. About the time you catch up financially, some unexpected circumstance knocks you back — to start over. The prophet Haggai described God's people that way: No matter what they did, they could never make ends meet. They never "got ahead." Do you feel like you *"earn wages, only to put them in a purse with holes in it?"*

A study of Haggai 1:6-14 finds God calling His people into account because they were neglecting His house in order to furnish their own homes first. He objected, because He is *preeminent*, meaning He takes first place over all things. Unpleasant consequences followed the Israelites' decision to neglect giving to God's work. Indeed, living outside of God's will is extremely difficult, exhausting, and very much like a fish swimming upstream.

Week 3

Day 4

Devotional *continued...*

There are both financial and spiritual consequences to harboring a skimpy attitude about giving to God's work. Setbacks will show up in your bank account. The testimony of tithing is that, by obeying God, 90 percent of your income blessed by God will last longer than spending 100 percent of your income without His blessing. Malachi 3:11 states that God opens a new degree of protection over us, including economically, when we honor Him in tithing. Choosing not to give, for whatever reason, limits God's ability to bless you. Is that what you want?

There also are spiritual consequences of not giving. In Luke 16:11, Jesus made it clear that you must first be trustworthy with worldly wealth if you want to be entrusted with deeper spiritual insights. That means you must demonstrate to God that you will faithfully use all your material assets—not just the tithe—to glorify His name. Further, Jesus states in John 14:21 that He will disclose more of Himself to those who first obey Him. Thus, the way you manage your material resources directly relates to your spiritual growth! By giving, you become a modern-day Abraham or Moses, embarking on a journey of faith with God as your Shepherd and Provider.

So, are you following His lead today or just thinking about it? The choice is yours: obey or disobey, follow Him or wait, commit or vacillate. You can experience His full blessing and protection or just get a taste of what could be. How will you handle your resources differently from this day forward because you belong to Jesus Christ?

Interactive — Week 3, Day 4

The third paragraph in the Devotional you just read mentions God's preeminence — His taking first place in all things. Does He truly have first place in Your life?

Examine the following case studies. In the spaces following them, describe what each person would need to do in order to give God preeminence.

Case Study 1: Sally is an inveterate catalog shopper. Often she orders things for her home because she can't resist the tempting photos. She and her husband promise they will give more faithfully to their church, but when time comes to write their contribution check, their bank account is in the red.

_____

_____

Case Study 2: Rich and his wife quarrel often over why they are unable to give to God's work. Rich is a soft touch when his family members plea for new clothes or other "things." He fears his wife and children will hate him if he tells them "no."

_____

_____

Case Study 3: Maria has large, unpaid college loans and a big note on a new car. Her friends pressure her to accompany them on a cruise. As a youth, Maria had learned to tithe. She feels guilty not continuing to do so. But she tells herself she deserves her fun, too.

_____

_____

To give God first place, Sally could toss out her catalogs when they arrive in the mail and ask the companies to remove her from their lists. Rich could rely on God's power to set boundaries, realizing the best gift he can give his family is the example of managing money soundly. Maria could set out on a program of debt reduction and could curtail spending, setting aside income for God.

Interactive — Week 3, Day 4

Can you testify to a time in which you were blessed because you were obedient to God in your tithing? If so, describe below. If tithing is not a practice with you and you are unable to answer this question, ask a Christian friend to share his/her tithing testimony with you. Write it here.

_____

_____

_____

Answer the last question posed in the Devotional. How will you handle your resources differently from this day forward?

_____

_____

_____

Below write out a brief prayer, asking God to help you with the commitment you just described.

_____

_____

_____

How do you demonstrate that you are trustworthy with your resources? Below, check all the ways that apply to you. Put a star by areas in which you'd like to improve.

- ❑ shopping sales rather than paying full price for items
- ❑ using cents-off coupons or rebates for purchases
- ❑ using a cash-only system for weekly expenses
- ❑ conducting family councils to prioritize individual needs
- ❑ strategic budgeting and living within my income
- ❑ other _____

List here a Scripture verse that may have helped guide you in your giving. Share this verse with someone in your family.

_____

_____

Devotional
Week 3, Day 5

This Week's Lessons

Day 1 : What should I give?

Day 2 : Why can't I give more?

Day 3 : Do I really trust God to meet my needs?

Day 4 : What if I choose not to give?

Day 5 : Why should I give sacrificially?

Day 6 : Why is the tithe holy?

Day 7 : Why are some biblical guidelines for giving?

Memory Verse

"But the king replied to Araunah, 'No I insist on paying you for it. I will not sacrifice to the Lord my God burnt offerings that cost me nothing."

-2 Samuel 24:24

Why Should I Give Sacrificially?

"But the king replied to Araunah, 'No I insist on paying you for it. I will not sacrifice to the Lord my God burnt offerings that cost me nothing."

(2 Samuel 24:24)

Everyone loves a bargain. That's why sales, outlet malls, yard sales, and flea markets are so popular. We're motivated to buy something for less than its retail value.

King David's example stands in sharp contrast to the "get something for nothing" mentality. When offered the threshing floor from Araunah for free, David insisted on paying for it. Why? Wouldn't good stewardship dictate that he take what he could get for free?

David sought to change God's mind regarding the plague that had come upon Israel, killing thousands. Nothing less than a genuine, heartfelt appeal before God would suffice. David realized that God wasn't impressed with offerings that didn't spring from heartfelt worship. Years later, Jesus admonished the scribes and Pharisees with these words from the prophet Isaiah, *"These people honor me with their lips, but their hearts are far from me"* (Matthew 15:8). Does your giving to God cost you anything?

Sacrifice means yielding something that is valuable to you in order to gain something of greater value. Sacrificial giving beckons you beyond the minimum standards of giving, such as tithing, to experience giving until it really hurts. The apostle Paul exclaimed, *"But whatever was to my profit I now consider loss for the sake of Christ"* (Philippians 3:7).

Week 3

Day 5

Devotional *continued...*

Sacrifice is the norm, not the exception, and it describes the lifestyle that Jesus calls His disciples to follow. He said, *"If anyone would come after me, he must deny himself and take up his cross and follow me"* (Matthew 16:24). You may sacrificially relinquish a desire, such as a brand new automobile, and purchase an older model so you can make more money available for reducing your church's building fund debt. Or, you may sacrifice a week of family vacation to go on a short-term, cross-cultural mission trip.

When was the last time you sacrificed something so you could give more generously to God's work? Can you think of something specific that you've given up recently? a vacation? eating out frequently? designer clothes or jewelry?

If God is to bring revival to our churches nationwide, we must crucify the attitude of doing just enough to get by in our churches. Our nation desperately needs men and women of God who are willing to boldly stand for Christ, no matter the cost. People who are looking for spiritual shortcuts and ways to minimize their investment in Christ will become spectators, rather than spiritual leaders on the cutting edge of God's work. King David wasn't hunting for a bargain; rather, he eagerly sought to please God with the finest he had to offer. Nothing less would suffice for him.

Aren't you thankful that God sacrificially offered His very best at the cross, to purchase peace and pardon for you through the shed blood of Jesus? Are His ways also your ways?

Interactive — Week 3, Day 5

Reread the quote from Matthew 15:8, in the third paragraph of your Devotional. Can you think of a time in which you claimed to be a follower of Christ but you failed to demonstrate it? If so, describe below.

_____

_____

You might recall a time in which you were a "Sunday-only" Christian — your lifestyle at work or at school didn't distinguish you from the unbelieving world. Your language or your thought life may have missed God's standard. Perhaps you treated others hurtfully or were insensitive.

As you just read, your giving to God also can reflect that you love the Lord with all your heart, even to the point of sacrifice.

Below, describe a time when your giving was perfunctory — the minimum to get by — perhaps just to clear your conscience, but without any sacrifice on your part.

_____

_____

This may have meant merely emptying your pocket change into an offering envelope, giving to God sporadically, or some sort of legalistic giving that conforms to the letter of the law but involves no real sacrifice on your part. If we're truthful, most of us can look back on those times when giving has been without any real cost.

Can you remember a time when your giving involved sacrifice — the type of "giving until it really hurt" that the Devotional mentioned? If so, describe below.

_____

_____

Reread Matthew 16:24. Underline the three requirements of discipleship that Jesus named in this verse. Describe something that you have denied yourself for the cause of Christ. It might be one of the items paragraph 6 mentions or some other act of self-denial you have made.

_____

_____

Interactive — Week 3, Day 5

Now describe what happened as a result of your sacrifice. How did God bless you? What lesson did you learn?

_____

_____

Read aloud this sentence from your Day 5 Devotional: "Our nation desperately needs men and women of God who are willing to boldly stand for Christ, no matter the cost." When is the last time you boldly took a stand for Christ that cost you?

_____

_____

Are you willing to endure lifted eyebrows because you take a stand when your lifestyle reflects fiscal responsibility? It happens! Some people might jibe you, "You can afford to live a little! Why do you drive that older model car?" Or, "Why do you carry that calculator in the supermarket? You don't have to worry about what you spend on groceries." When you take a stand for Christ and manage your resources so that you can give sacrificially, people won't always understand. But the contentment that occurs when you follow Christ is unparalleled.

If you are married, go "knee to knee" with your spouse in prayer. Turn your chairs so your knees touch. Clasp both hands. If you are single, join a friend for prayer time. Talk with your partner about ways you feel the Lord might be speaking to you to give sacrificially. Then spend some time praying about what God has put on your heart.

Devotional
Week 3, Day 6

Memory Verse

"A tithe of everything from the land, whether grain from the soil or fruit from the trees, belongs to the Lord; it is holy to the Lord."

-Leviticus 27:30

Why Is the Tithe Holy?

"A tithe of everything from the land, whether grain from the soil or fruit from the trees, belongs to the Lord; it is holy to the Lord." (Leviticus 27:30)

Picture yourself at one of those scrumptious church suppers: Your plate is loaded with fried chicken, casseroles, and vegetables — all of your favorites. Your dessert plate has not one, but two, generous slices of pie — and a brownie, of course.

Just as you spread your napkin in your lap, the unthinkable happens. The person seated next to you reaches his fork over into your plate and begins to help himself to YOUR food — mind you, without the courtesy of asking permission. No doubt, you would be offended since, in America, the food on your plate is regarded as your property.

When the word *holy* appears in Scripture, it describes something sanctified or set apart for a specific purpose, such as people or items. The Bible says the tithe is holy to God, meaning it belongs to Him. The 10 percent of all your increase (the tithe) isn't yours to spend. You'd be offended by someone eating off your plate without permission. Do you suppose God is any less offended when we dip into His portion to pay for our wants and desires?

According to the Barna Research Group, Ltd., barely over half (55 percent) of people attending Baptist churches during a typical month give anything to the church, much less tithe. Only 3 to 5 percent of American Christians actually tithe, depending on the church denomination.[1] Just imagine all that could be accomplished in Jesus' name if all of your church family respected the tithe as holy to the Lord.

Week 3

Day 6

Devotional *continued...*

It's a mistake to live your lifestyle at the expense of what rightfully belongs to the Lord: the tithe. Not only will you be weak spiritually as a result, but your church will be weakened by a lack of resources.

What can you do if you're giving less than a tithe? Since tithing is a worship matter of the heart and not simply an accounting function, begin with your heart attitude. Do you *want* to honor God by tithing? If not, confess that attitude. Ask God to create in you a generous, cheerful attitude about tithing. Remember, He's not impressed with your dollars; He's impressed with the worshipful attitude of your heart.

Next, to determine areas of overspending, review your budget. Ask yourself what areas you can reduce in order to increase your giving to a tithe. Then pray for God to give you strength to make these lifestyle adjustments.

Finally, seal your commitment in an act of family worship. Teach your children to understand that your decision to tithe is an act of *faith*, designed to honor God. If you don't have immediate family with whom to share, tell a close friend about your decision. Then watch for God to bless you beyond your imagination (see Malachi 3:10, Ephesians 3:20-21).

[1] George Barna, *How to Increase Giving in Your Church* (Ventura: Regal Books, 1997) 20, 178.

What Are Some Biblical Guidelines for Giving?

"Each man should give what he has decided in his heart to give, not reluctantly or under compulsion, for God loves a cheerful giver." (2 Corinthians 9:7)

This Week's Lessons

Memory Verse

"Each man should give what he has decided in his heart to give, not reluctantly or under compulsion, for God loves a cheerful giver."
-2 Corinthians 9:7

Does this routine sound familiar? "Bless both the gift and the giver, in Jesus' name. Amen." Following the offertory prayer, the scramble is on to prepare your check before the offering plates arrive. Quick, find the checkbook, check your balance, decide how much to give, write the check and sign it before the offering plate reaches you. Whew! Miracles do happen! If that describes your method of giving, God's Word offers a better plan.

The apostle Paul says that giving to God's work should be planned and not haphazard. *"Each man should give what he has decided in his heart to give"* (2 Corinthians 9:7). Rather than waiting for the middle of a church service to write the offering check, why not do it in advance? Suppose $500 a month represents your tithe to God's work. In a four-Sunday month, you could write a check each Sunday before the service for $125. During a five-Sunday month, the checks would be for $100. It's that simple, but you have to commit to a plan for giving — a step that requires both discipline and commitment.

To maintain your plan, you have to live within your means by not overspending in other areas of your budget. Make your commitment to give to God's work first, and then arrange your expenditures around that commitment. If you have a plan for giving, you should have a solid estimate of how much you'll give to God's work through the end of the year, assuming that your income remains the same. Giving shouldn't be a matter of guesswork.

Week 3

Day 7

Devotional *continued...*

Paul also says that we are not to give *"reluctantly or under compulsion."* If you have resentment or regret in your heart when you give, Paul says you're missing the point. God isn't a divine accountant, attempting to squeeze every possible dime out of you. You might find some resentment in your heart when you give money that could be used to pay bills. If that's true, I suggest you confess that to God. Just tell Him, "God, I need your help. Forgive me for my resentment. Create a new attitude and joy in me as I give to Your work." Make that a persistent prayer and He will transform Your attitude.

We must not give grudgingly or under compulsion, because *"God loves a cheerful giver."* He delights in people who give as He does: cheerfully and generously!

As an act of worship, giving may be one of the most exciting aspects of your worship service today. So prayerfully prepare to worship God with your offering. When you give,

> Create a plan and follow it
> Don't give grudgingly or under compulsion
> Give cheerfully, because that's the way God gives!

Devotional
Week 4, Day 1

Memory Verse

"He who loves pleasure will become poor; whoever loves wine and oil will never be rich."

-Proverbs 21:17

Why Can't I Save Money?
"He who loves pleasure will become poor; whoever loves wine and oil will never be rich." (Proverbs 21:17)

It may strike you as odd to contemplate saving money after we just talked about the theme of giving last week. But, in the long run, a lifestyle of saving will help you to give even more to others. Saving promotes giving!

Everyone can save money. Even a small amount adds up over time. Most people don't save because they consistently spend all of their income — and then some. As a nation, we're saving less money now than since the Great Depression of the 1930s.

Start by making a commitment to save. Abandon the idea that you are at liberty to spend everything that you make. You might find it helpful to have money withheld from your income just as you do for taxes. Resolve in your heart that you will save something from every pay period; then build your lifestyle and subsequent expenditures around your commitment.

Saving money is a spiritual issue, because it requires discipline and control of your desires and impulses. In fact, the key to saving money is self-control, which is listed among the fruits of the Holy Spirit in Galatians 5:22-23. King Solomon accurately described the person who lacks self-control: *"Like a city whose walls are broken down is a man who lacks self-control"* (Proverbs 25:28). In ancient days, a city without walls was subject to any intruders who passed by and was thus in a state of constant disarray. Without self-control, your finances will dictate your decisions, instead of vice versa. Sales, bargains, and an insatiable desire for more things will consume all of your income and more! As the verse says, *"He who loves pleasure will become poor"* (Proverbs 21:17).

Week 4

Day 1

Devotional *continued...*

Most people who struggle to start saving make the mistake of maintaining their current standard of living while trying to squeeze saving into the budget — if they're even on a budget. But that presumes there is already leftover money in your monthly cash flow, which usually isn't the case. If that's your situation, you must decide how to cut back your lifestyle to open up cash flow for savings.

Finally, ask God to create a heart of contentment in you. Contentment is finding God's plan for you and experiencing His peace to live that plan. That's why the apostle Paul was able to state, *"I have learned to be content whatever the circumstances. I know what it is to be in need, and I know what it is to have plenty. I have learned the secret of being content in any and every situation, whether well fed or hungry, whether living in plenty or in want. I can do everything through Him who gives me strength"* (Philippians 4:11-13).

I believe God is calling His church to experience a resurgence of self-control, peace, and contentment. With those qualities present and growing in your life, saving money will become a natural consequence. Are you among those responding to His call?

Interactive — Week 4, Day 1

The first paragraph of your Devotional states that a lifestyle of saving will enable you to give even more to others. Below, describe a time in your life when you have found this to be true.

_____

_____

You might have recalled times as a child when you kept a jar full of coins that you saved up for a missions offering or a special worthy cause. As an adult, you might have set aside money, over and above your tithe, for a church building fund or benevolent fund. Ideally, at such times, the value of putting money away for causes outside your own immediate wants proved to be a meaningful discipline.

Have you ever believed that you must spend everything you make?

❑ Yes ❑ No

If you answered "Yes," what impact did this practice have on your life?

_____

_____

Spending all you make and more can leave you temporarily satisfied with the things you acquire, but long term, it can cause you to feel hopeless and helpless as you realize you have no reserve on which to draw. The material wealth you acquire becomes the rudder that steers the ship instead of the contentment of knowing that you are prepared for the unexpected _"with your cloak tucked into your belt, your sandals on your feet and your staff in your hand"_ (Exodus 12:11).

In what areas of your life do you believe you demonstrate self-control? (Check all that apply.)

❑ I refrain from saying hurtful things to people.
❑ I restrain myself from eating harmful food.
❑ I have a disciplined exercise plan.
❑ I contain my desire to acquire more and more things.
❑ I budget my time to fit my priorities.
❑ I resist in the area of sexual temptation.
❑ Other _____

Go back a᛫ ¹ put a star by the area you consider the most challenging for you.

You may not have readily associated the area of saving money (or even some of the other areas mentioned) with spiritual issues, but the Devotional stresses that self-control (which includes a broad spectrum of disciplines) is indeed a fruit of the Spirit. Perhaps it will help you to remember this the next time you're tempted to spend as though you are a "city without walls."

Have you experienced a time in which out-of-control finances dictated your decisions? If so, describe below. (Example: I needed to make a job change because of an abusive boss, but I was unable to do so because heavy debt kept me tied to my paycheck.)

_____

_____

_____

_____

_____

The Devotional suggests that you may need to cut back your lifestyle to open up cash flow for savings. As you prayerfully consider whether this is a need you have, think of ways you might accomplish this. Below, list four areas in which you might cut back or reallocate resources.

_____

_____

_____

_____

_____

Stop and pray, asking God to give you the heart of contentment the Devotional mentions. Ask Him to help you be content with the blessings of life that money can't buy. Ask Him to help you make Paul's statement in Philippians 4:11-13 your creed as it relates to the acquisition things.

Devotional
Week 4, Day 2

Memory Verse

"And God is able to make all grace abound to you, so that in all things at all times, having all that you need, you will abound in every good work."

-2 Corinthians 9:8

What's the Purpose of Saving?

"And God is able to make all grace abound to you, so that in all things at all times, having all that you need, you will abound in every good work."

(2 Corinthians 9:8)

Does saving money demonstrate a lack of faith that God will provide for your needs? Does saving violate what Jesus taught: *"Do not store up for yourselves treasures on earth, where moth and rust destroy, and where thieves break in and steal"* (Matthew 6:19)? To the contrary, I believe saving money fulfills God's will when we do it with a pure motive.

Saving money as a lifestyle fulfills all three of the objectives related in the 2 Corinthians verse above. First, accumulating a surplus of money is a testimony that the God of the Bible faithfully will meet your needs. We undermine that witness when bills become past due, money runs out before the end of the month, and creditors form a negative opinion of you and your lifestyle. Carefully monitor your lifestyle so your abundance doesn't get squandered on things you don't really need.

The second objective for saving is to accumulate extra money for emergency or unexpected expenses. I promise you that automobiles will eventually wear out, require new tires, and occasionally require a mechanic's touch. Your home and appliances will require periodic repairs also. During this next year, thousands of people — Christians included — will become ill and require medical attention. Thousands more will joyously discover that they have a new baby on the way. Because these situations are so predictable, they can hardly be called emergencies or surprises. The question is, are you preparing financially for these possibilities? My recommendation is that, as

Week 4

Day 2

Devotional *continued...*

a minimum goal, you save between three and six months of your income in a contingency fund. By taking this step of preparation, you will experience this element of God's purpose in saving: *"in all things at all times, having all that you need."*

Finally, God desires for you to accumulate a surplus to share with others. Few things are as disheartening as learning of a person's need and realizing that the money you could have shared has been squandered on something that proved to be insignificant. God has a wiser plan for you according to the apostle Paul: *"At the present time your plenty will supply what they need, so that in turn their plenty will supply what you need"* (2 Corinthians 8:14). That biblical principle provides the foundation for the entire insurance industry. You contribute premiums to the insurance company, creating a huge reservoir of money. When you have a claim, you gain access to the money you need.

The same idea applies in the Christian life. God raises up some people in the church with an abundance and others with needs. Sharing the surplus with those in need demonstrates His love. Through your abundance, you're prepared to *"abound in every good work."*

Have you made systematic saving part of your lifestyle? If not, when you will start?

Interactive — Week 4, Day 2

Read the following case studies. Put a plus sign (+) by any that you believe demonstrate saving with a pure motive and a minus sign (-) by any that represent saving with an impure motive. Put an asterisk (*) by any motive that you've used.

1. Mike's aunt bought him a new car for graduation. Although it was an adequate car for his needs, he drove it grudgingly because it was not a trendy model like his friends owned. As soon as he got a job, he began a rigorous savings plan to buy a new one.

2. Sandy and Mac had rented an apartment for years while they saved their money for a home purchase. Although they could have bought one long before, they waited and saved until they could make a size-able down payment so their monthly payments were not a financial burden to them.

3. Angie heard a missionary speak about how volunteer mission teams were needed to reach the people of her country for Christ. Angie began setting aside part of her paycheck every month with the goal of paying her way on a mission trip in two years.

Ideally you answered that the last two illustrations mentioned savings plans with the pure motives. Savings in the first instance was motivated by greed.

The Devotional notes that 2 Corinthians 9:8 shows God's three purposes for your saving:

1. It demonstrates that God meets needs.
2. It provides for unexpected or emergency expenses.
3. It enables you to share through your abundance and to respond freely to His prompting.

Go back and put an asterisk by the above category to which you can most readily relate, based on your experience with savings. Then below, describe why.

_____

_____

_____

Has your witness for Christ ever been undermined because you failed to demonstrate financial responsibility?

❏ Yes   ❏ No

If you answered "yes," describe how this happened. (Example: I tried to witness to my neighbors by taking them tracts and inviting them to attend church with me. Then, because of poor financial management, our utilities were cut off for a time, and several neighbors knew this. I felt we looked hypocritical because we had not been good financial stewards of what God had given us.)

_____

_____

_____

How do you respond to the Devotional's suggestion that you save between 3-6 months of income in a contingency fund for emergency needs?

_____

_____

_____

What steps would be necessary for you to do this, if you do not make this a practice already?

_____

_____

_____

Share with your spouse how you feel about the concepts posed in the Day 2 Devotional. Discuss a time when you've felt really good about your savings strategy. Discuss a time when your failure to save has impacted your marriage seriously. Compare each other's answers on the question about the 3-6 month contingency fund. Together, make a list that you can agree on as savings goals. If you are single, share your answers to these questions with a trusted friend.

Devotional
Week 4, Day 3

Memory Verse

"Go to the ant, you sluggard; consider its ways and be wise! It has no commander, no overseer or ruler, yet it stores its provisions in summer and gathers its food at harvest."

-Proverbs 6:6-8

What Is a Good Plan for Saving?

"Go to the ant, you sluggard; consider its ways and be wise! It has no comman-der, no overseer or ruler, yet it stores its provisions in summer and gathers its food at harvest." (Proverbs 6:6-8)

God's creation is marked by orderliness. Scientists know exactly when lunar and solar eclipses will occur, how to chart high and low tides around the world, and precisely how many trillions of miles (5,878) light travels in a year. My work at Cape Canaveral back in the 1960s depended upon God's orderly creation. So it is no surprise that saving money requires a plan, since saving depends on your ability to control spending. God even uses ants to illustrate the wisdom and orderliness of saving. You will never be able to save unless you consistently spend less than you earn. Do you have a plan yet?

A spending plan for an entire year is called an annual budget; dividing that plan by twelve months creates a monthly budget. Consistent saving will be impossible without a clear plan to control spending. If you're over-spending, maintaining a budget will help to identify exactly what habits are causing the overspending. Armed with that knowledge, you can make the necessary changes to prevent deeper debt. Although a budget is primarily a plan to manage expenditures, it also provides structure for your savings plan.

To develop a realistic savings plan, begin by identifying the areas of your budget that are most vulnerable to emergencies — things you wouldn't normally cover with your monthly cash flow. Typical categories would include automobile repair, house repairs, and medical expenses. Develop a spreadsheet with a column for each of these categories, thus allowing you to track the amount of money available in each category.

Week 4

Day 3

Devotional *continued...*

Also include categories in which expenses occur sporadically, such as life insurance, car insurance, and the clothing categories. Your total deposit to savings may be only $75 or $100, with that amount broken into subcategories: clothing, medical, car repairs, and so on.

Another effective way to save is to have money withheld from your paycheck. Like the ants of Proverbs 6, lay aside some of what you receive today for projected needs in the future. Most people avoid tax problems because Uncle Sam just takes his share out of your check first. Since that money is already gone from your check, you've learned to make necessary lifestyle adjustments. You can do the same by having savings withheld, such as through a 401(K) or 403(B) savings plan. Occasionally employers even offer matching money, to encourage you to contribute to that plan. Check with the financial officer at your office to get the details. Since these are retirement plans, there will be restrictions on having access to the money. Nonetheless, it may be the perfect savings plan for you.

A keen insight is found in the way that God created ants. If He created them to gather provisions in the summer for the cold winter, can His will for you to save be any less wise?

Interactive — Week 4, Day 3

How do you feel about developing a plan for savings like the one described in the Devotional? (Check all the statements that apply.)

❑ I'm not a very orderly person. Doing things systematically is difficult for me.

❑ It's too tough for me to control my spending. I try to stay flexible and not rigid.

❑ I can't develop a plan because I feel too guilt-riddled if I stray from it.

❑ I've tried for years to spend less than I earn, and it can't be done.

❑ I'd like to live this way and believe I can, by God's power.

❑ Other _____

Regardless of whether you have a bent toward disorderliness or whether you've struggled in the savings area, getting your spending and savings plan under control is entirely possible. Just as the Scripture indicates that God created ants to store provisions for winter, God can help you manage your resources for the future in a way that pleases Him. Even if you've tried in the past and strayed, God can help you bring your spending/savings patterns back in line.

Describe a time when you believe you've been the most effective at controlling spending and maintaining a budget.

_____

_____

_____

What tenets did you use then that would help you now? What tactics worked that you believe you could try again if you want to improve your savings plan?

_____

_____

_____

You might have mentioned that, in the past, you were able to set aside money regularly to give to the church, even if you were unable to remain disciplined in other areas. You might have had a period in which you locked up credit cards and used only cash for your weekly purchases, such as gasoline. You might have set aside money throughout the year for Christmas gift purchases rather than running the risk of overspending at holiday time.

If you can look back at past successes and target what worked for you at one time, you have a proven foundation on which to build, even if you generally believe that disciplined spending and savings are impossible for you.

Take some of the steps that the Devotional outlined. If you believe you are operating under a workable budget already, examine it and see if some areas still exist where you'd like to improve. For example, you may decide that you would like to step up a plan for debt reduction, with an accelerated payoff date in one year instead of 18 months.

Identify your emergency areas (car repair, broken appliances, etc.) and begin tracking the amount of money available for them. How much do you need to save in order to cover those expenses?

_____
_____
_____

How can you reach this savings goal? What other budgetary reductions might you have to make in order to free up money for these savings?

_____
_____
_____
_____

How much do you have withheld for retirement through a 401(K), 403(B) or other saving plan?

_____
_____

Are there other ways for you to have money withheld for your savings? Brainstorm about a few of them here.

_____
_____
_____
_____

Devotional
Week 4, Day 4

Memory Verse

"Instruct those who are rich in this present world not to be conceited or to fix their hope on the uncertainties of riches, but on God, who richly supplies us with all things to enjoy. Instruct them to do good, to be rich in good works, to be generous and ready to share, storing up for themselves the treasure of a good foundation for the future, so that they may take hold of that which is life indeed."

-1 Timothy 6:17-19

Am I Saving or Am I Hoarding?

"Instruct those who are rich in this present world not to be conceited or to fix their hope on the uncertainty of riches, but on God, who richly supplies us with all things to enjoy. Instruct them to do good, to be rich in good works, to be generous and ready to share, storing up for themselves the treasure of a good foundation for the future, so that they may take hold of that which is life indeed." (1 Timothy 6:17-19, NASB)

It isn't a sin to be wealthy in material goods. The apostle Paul didn't teach people who are rich to feel guilty, repent, and give all their money away, as if it were a particular virtue to be poor. Rather, his directives to Timothy describe how to act with an abundance. The problem, so to speak, is not as much your checking account as it is the integrity of your heart. Your motives will determine whether you are righteously and prudently saving money, or hoarding.

Telltale signs of hoarding are that you won't spend savings, even when a need arises, or that you always need more to be "safe." Notice how these traits contradict the principle of trusting God. Hoarding is a lifestyle driven to amass more and more material goods, believing that security is to be found in such things.

Further, hoarders use wealth to distinguish themselves as being better than other human beings. Money and material goods become a measure of pride in oneself, exemplified in King Nebuchadnezzar's attitude when he once reflected, *"Is not this the great Babylon I have built as the royal residence, by my mighty power and for the glory of my majesty?"* (Daniel 4:30). In contrast, Jesus taught that *"a man's life does not consist in the abundance of his possessions"* (Luke 12:15).

Week 4

Day 4

Devotional *continued...*

Saving is clearly different than hoarding; people who are righteously saving recognize that they are stewards, not owners of material goods. Like Paul, they can live with or without them (Philippians 4:12). More importantly, their lives are committed to using their resources for God's purposes — seeing the nations come to Christ! In that spirit, Paul admonished the Corinthians, *"On the first day of the week, each one of you should set aside a sum of money in keeping with his income, saving it up, so that when I come no collections will have to be made"* (1 Corinthians 16:2). Saving with a Godly motive is both a responsible and prudent way to live. Your discipline and wise living will bless your life, and the lives of others.

Distinguishing between saving and hoarding can be symbolized by the human hand. Those who hoard desperately clutch all they can hold in a closed fist. Prudent savers, like Jesus, display an open palm — open to sharing God's abundance with whomever He would desire and however it would please Him. That requires sacrifice, just as when the open hands of Jesus were nailed to a cross.

Which hand best describes you — clenched or open?

Interactive — Week 4, Day 4

In 1 Timothy 6:17-19, what did Paul instruct Timothy to tell those who had abundance?

- ❑ Confess their sins for having too much wealth.
- ❑ Fix their hope on God.
- ❑ Give all their money away out of guilt.

The Bible does not condemn those with abundance or suggest that they give it all away. It urges people to be content with what they have and look to God rather than to things as their source of hope.

Reread paragraphs two and three, where the Devotional reveals various characteristics of hoarding.

Have you ever —

. . . refused to spend savings, even when some obvious need arose, because you felt it was unsafe not to hang on to every penny of it?

❑ Yes   ❑ No

. . . believed you must acquire more and more in order to be safe?

❑ Yes   ❑ No

. . . desired to accumulate wealth so you could look better than others?

❑ Yes   ❑ No

Read the following case studies and put an "S" by the saver illustrations and an "H" by the hoarding illustrations.

Chuck kept six months of savings in a special account as an "insurance policy." Then, when his air-conditioner went out during the peak of the summer heat, he risked his health rather than spend his savings for repairs.

Anita believed in stockpiling canned goods on her shelves. Her neighbor lost her job and couldn't buy groceries. Because she was afraid she wouldn't be safe otherwise, Anita refused to share her food with the neighbor.

Clark loved to brag to others about the size of his bank account. He boasted to his co-workers about how his "bottom line" was increasing. He was the only person in his office who refused to contribute to a love offering when a co-worker lost his home in a fire.

Can you relate to any of the case studies you just read? (I hope you recognized that all of these were hoarders, without a saver in the group.) Below, write your own testimony about a time in which you clenched all you had with a closed fist instead of sharing with others.

_____
_____
_____
_____

How about the opposite — saving with an open hand? Describe a time in which your disciplined savings blessed others.

_____
_____
_____
_____

Are you truly using your resources for God's purposes—to see the nations come to Christ? Consider using your resources in one of these ways. (Check any areas where you will commit to giving, or where you give already.)

- ❑ Giving to missions, or increasing what you already give for this purpose
- ❑ Helping your church buy supplies to send on mission trips
- ❑ Contributing to buy Bibles for people who have none
- ❑ Contributing supplies for backyard Bible clubs your church sponsors
- ❑ Other _____

How do you act with abundance? Ask God to search your heart and show you whether you are finding your security in things. Ask Him to show you how you can be a part of what Isaiah 52:10 mentions when it proclaims that *"all the ends of the earth will see the salvation of our God."*

Devotional
Week 4, Day 5

Memory Verse

"Do not weary yourself to gain wealth, Cease from your consideration of it. When you set your eyes on it, it is gone. For wealth certainly makes itself wings, Like an eagle that flies toward the heavens."

-Proverbs 23:4-5

How Much Is Enough?

"Do not weary yourself to gain wealth, cease from your consideration of it. When you set your eyes on it, it is gone. For wealth certainly makes itself wings, Like an eagle that flies toward the heavens." (Proverbs 23:4-5, NASB)

Do you plan to leave your children an inheritance? How can you know how much to save if you plan to retire early? How can you count on investments when the stock market has such inexplicable rallies and declines? Questions like these press the issue of, "How much is enough?"

Answers will vary for each family. For instance, if asked how many bricks it would take to build a home, you'd first have to understand what size the builder planned for the house to be. You can't answer *"How much is enough?"* without some understanding of God's plan for your life. Variables will include the size of your family, how much formal education is in your future, your health, your standard of living, and so on. Those factors are highly personal, but there are key biblical principles to shape your answers to the question, *"How much is enough?"*

God owns everything (Psalm 24:1). Don't attempt to compete with Him for ownership of *things*, much less your *life*. Submit to Him in genuine obedience and, like the widow of Zarephath (1 Kings 17:16), His provision will always be sufficient for you. Such a lifestyle is much different than that of people who frantically trying to protect themselves from future unknowns; they will never get enough.

Week 4
Day 5

Devotional *continued...*

God promises to meet your needs (Philippians 4:19). Be careful, since what you regard as a necessity God may see as surplus in your lifestyle. Distinguish your needs from your wants and desires, since God may plan to meet the needs of others with what you're holding as surplus. That's why Jesus said it is hard for a rich man to enter the kingdom of heaven — it takes great spiritual discernment to prevent being led astray!

God can use money to open or to close doors of opportunity. Don't waste time amassing resources for an opportunity that is contrary to God's will. Remember, if He says "no" to one opportunity, He has something even better in mind for you. Be patient; when God calls His people to a task, He supplies what is needed (Hebrews 13:20-21, Philippians 4:19).

The only instance of retirement in Scripture tells of Levites retiring from temple service at the age of 50. Retirement for God's people should mean saving in order to serve without a salary. All too often retirement equates to rusting away.

Having enough means prudently preparing for the future while you are depending on God. If you no longer depend on Him, you will miss His will. God delights in performing the impossible for those who trust Him (2 Chronicles 16:9).

How much is enough? Your answer comes on the exciting journey of faith that God calls you to experience with Him.

Interactive — Week 4, Day 5

The Scripture passage for today urges you to not "weary yourself to gain wealth."
Can you think of a time in which you have done that? Below, check any descriptions that apply to you.

- ❏ I worked overtime in order to provide materially for my family; now I
  see that my family needed my presence more.
- ❏ I hoarded money selfishly when I needed to use that money to serve
  God.
- ❏ I saved for a larger home than I actually needed in order to live in a
  high-status part of town. I now realize that God desired me to make a
  wiser choice.
- ❏ Other _____

The "How much is enough?" question is one you can apply to almost any
purchase you make and almost any plan that you have that involves money.
Another way to consider this matter is to ask yourself, "Will God be pleased
with this choice I'm making right now regarding finances?"

What are some variables that you need to consider when answering the question,
"How much is enough?" Check any below that apply to you, or supply your own
answer.

- ❏ I am the sole support of aging relatives.
- ❏ I have a dependent who is developmentally challenged and can never be
  a wage earner.
- ❏ I am single and the sole support of myself.
- ❏ I have a physical condition that may make early retirement necessary.
- ❏ I had a financial reversal that kept me from saving for retirement earlier.
- ❏ Other _____

Has there been a time in which you saved money for an opportunity, only to see
God close the door because it was contrary to His will? If so, describe below.

_____

_____

_____

_____

Interactive — Week 4, Day 5

When has He called you to a task and then graciously supplied what was needed to perform that task?

_____

_____

_____

Missionary stories on this order are legendary. An individual feels called to go on a volunteer mission trip; someone supplies her with "frequent flyer" miles to fund an airplane ticket. A couple is led to surrender for career missions; buyers for their home and cars surface almost instantly. If you are moving within the center of God's will, He will provide what is necessary to make that task possible.

Have you ever stopped depending on God and missed His will? Below describe a time in which you tried to plan for the future without Him.

_____

_____

_____

Reread the Devotional paragraph on retirement. Do you believe retirement is a time to rust away, or do you see yourself continuing to "serve without a salary," as the Devotional describes? Below, jot down some ideas on retirement goals you have for yourself when you no longer work for pay. In what ways do you plan to continue to serve the Lord in those years?

_____

_____

_____

On a separate sheet of paper, write down some of the long-term ideas that came to mind as you've completed your Day 5 work. Keep that paper in your bill drawer or another place where you house financial documents. Ask God to keep you from being short-sighted. Pray in faith that He will supply what You need as you walk in the center of His will.

Devotional
Week 4, Day 6

Memory Verse

"Now finish the work, so that your eager willingness to do it may be matched by your completion of it, according to your means."

-2 Corinthians 8:11

How Can You Finish What You Start?

"Now finish the work, so that your eager willingness to do it may be matched by your completion of it, according to your means." (2 Corinthians 8:11)

Have you ever returned highly motivated from a conference or retreat, only to find yourself unable to keep the fires of enthusiasm burning? If so, you're not the first to experience a post-mountaintop letdown. Only hours after experiencing the glory of Jesus' transfiguration, the disciples were unable to cast out a demon from a boy (Matthew 17:14-16). The Corinthians desired to help the apostle Paul, but in the verse above Paul had to admonish them to finish the commitment they had made the previous year.

It's hard to keep new commitments. Over the last four weeks, I hope God has impressed you with new changes that will catapult you into new dimensions of spiritual growth. Like the Corinthians, your eager willingness must be matched by your completion of your new commitments to Christ. I offer you several insights to keep you on track.

First, you must walk in God's power. Paul used the example of the Macedonian church to stimulate the Corinthians to keep their commitments. In 2 Corinthians 8:5, he states, *". . . they gave themselves first to the Lord and then to us in keeping with God's will."* To be the man or woman of God that He desires, you must be saturated in His power — the power of the Holy Spirit. You cannot measure up to the challenges of today in your own strength.

Week 4
Day 6

Devotional *continued...*

Next, you must decide to act on what you know. Jesus said the wise man is one who *"hears these words of mine and puts them into practice"* (Matthew 7:24). Challenge yourself to summarize what the Spirit of God is saying to you and your church, and then act upon His leading! Be on a constant search for areas in which to grow, repent, and please God. What attitudes and behaviors is He calling you to forsake? What work is taking place in your life and your church *right now* that can be explained no other way except that God is doing it?

Finally, become accountable. Others must know of your new commitments and new zeal. I challenge your church family to new, unprecedented degrees of faithful stewardship. What He is doing in your church will be contagious. From there, He will stimulate "love and good deeds" in others, all to one end: that the world may hear the name of Jesus Christ. Jesus said, *"And this gospel of the kingdom will be preached in the whole world as a testimony to all nations, and then the end will come"* (Matthew 24:14).

Great moves of God begin with one person taking the first step of obedience in faith. Peter preached on the day of Pentecost (Acts 2). Paul wrote from prison (Philippians 1). History was changed. Can God count on you to complete the good work He has started in you (Philippians 1:6, 2:13)?

Devotional
Week 4, Day 7

Will You Accept the Goal of Stewardship?

"May God be gracious to us and bless us and make his face shine upon us; may your ways may be known on earth, your salvation among all nations."

(Psalm 67:1-2)

Memory Verse

"May God be gracious to us and bless us and make his face shine upon us; may your ways may be known on earth, your salvation among all nations."

-Psalm 67:1-2

Have you ever researched your family ancestry? As interesting as studying your family's genealogy is, tracking your *spiritual* family tree is even more intriguing. By that I mean tracing those who influenced you to come to faith in Jesus Christ. Was there one particular person who had the most direct influence on you to become a Christian — perhaps it was a parent, Sunday school teacher, youth leader or pastor?

But who influenced *that* person to accept Christ? Theoretically, you have a spiritual family tree that reaches all the way back to Acts 2 when the apostle Peter first preached the Gospel and 3,000 were saved!

Under the leading of the Holy Spirit, the Psalmist captured the full cycle of stewardship from God's perspective in Psalm 67. To paraphrase, God blesses you so you will bless others — even to the ends of the earth.

Through God's blessing, grace, and forgiveness, you have new life. He not only saves your soul for eternity (John 10:28), but He brings purpose to everyday living. The apostle Paul put it this way, *"And he died for all, that those who live should no longer live for themselves but for him who died for them and was raised again"* (2 Corinthians 5:15), and *"For we are God's workmanship, created in Christ Jesus to do good works, which God prepared in advance for us to do"* (Ephesians 2:10).

Week 4
Day 7

Devotional *continued...*

The testimony of Scripture is that you are the central focus of His love. If you were the only person on earth, Jesus still would have died and risen for you. But you're not the only person. You have about 5.5 billion neighbors, most of whom don't know Christ as Savior yet.

The goal of Christian stewardship is nothing more than using all the resources God has entrusted to your care — your time, talents, money, spiritual gifts, all that you are — to fulfill His will of reaching the nations for Christ. His Great Commission is directed to all people, including making His love real to orphans, the homeless, those in business, the single parent — all deserve to hear of God's love and saving grace. His plan includes working through you.

God says you are a caretaker, or steward, of the Gospel (1 Corinthians 4:1-2). You can touch people in your sphere of influence that others cannot reach. His Holy Spirit will do the convicting and converting (John 16:8-11); your role as a steward is to share the truth of His great love and plan of salvation. *The Gospel isn't yours to keep.*

Following my bout with cancer in 1995, I came to believe that God spared my life to maximize my opportunities to share His good news. I refuse to be the last link in the chain of my spiritual family. Will you be? Will God be able to say, *"Well done, good and faithful servant!"* (Matthew 25:21a) when you stand before Him?

Memory Verse

"Well, done, good and faithful servant!"

-Matthew 25:21a

How to Get Out of Debt
A Step-by-Step Approach

1. **Commit your situation to the Lord.** Joshua 24:15 carries the idea of coming to a deciding point. This is key. In the absence of a clear commitment to living by God's principles, people typically revert to old spending patterns once the "heat" is off and pressures let up. Ask yourself, "Is my goal to live for God and honor Him with all areas of my life, including my finances, or just to relieve the financial pressure by getting out of debt?"

2. **Begin to tithe.** It sounds like a contradiction to ask people to control spending by increasing their giving to the church to a minimum of 10 percent. The testimony of tithing is, however, that God will bless and enable you to stretch the 90 percent you keep and manage further than keeping 100 percent for yourself. That is precisely what happens when you obey God. A logical sequence for tithing is found in Scripture.

   a. Deuteronomy 14:22-23 teaches that one of the benefits of tithing is learning to fear (revere) the Lord. Fear does not mean cowering in His presence. By faith, tithing unleashes His divine power in our lives, enabling us to see His awesome power and care over our lives.

   b. According to Proverbs 9:10, the fear of the Lord is the beginning of wisdom. When it comes to acquiring wise strategies of managing money, you can choose the wisdom of the world (which James 3:15 calls demonic) or God's ways.

   c. If anyone needs wisdom, it's the person with bills stacking up, collection agencies calling, and too much month at the end of their money. True wisdom comes from God (James 1:5) and grows where the fear of the Lord is. Tithing fosters the fear of the Lord.

3. **Re-evaluate your needs, wants, and desires.** *"But I need this,"* we say to ourselves. Do you really need it? Or do you simply want it? You may need transportation, want a new car, and desire a new BMW.

How to Get Out of Debt

Our culture teaches us to strive to be pampered, that you deserve all the perks you can get your hands on, even if you can't afford them. And if you're consistently spending more money than you earn, you're living beyond the means God has supplied for you. Financial freedom results from experiencing contentment while living within the boundaries God has set for you. With a realistic view of your actual *needs*, follow these steps to maintain self-control and curtail spending.

- **Delay major purchases** for thirty days, if possible. With the passing of time, you may discover you didn't really need the item(s) after all.

- **Stay out of the mall.** An alcoholic will likely find it difficult to refrain from drinking if he or she spends idle time in a bar. If you habitually overspend, avoid malls and the stores where you typically spend money. The apostle Paul specifically reminds us in 1 Corinthians 10:13 that God will provide a way of escape in the midst of temptation. Become aware of what tempts you the most, and resist those scenarios with the strength of God (see James 4:7).

- **Exercise self-control in all areas of life.** Self-control is named as one of the fruits of the Holy Spirit in Galatians 5:23. If you struggle to maintain self-control over spending money, it is likely that you struggle with self-control in other areas of life as well, such as food, emotions, negative thought patterns, time management, or sexuality. Make self-control a focus for growth, and establish accountability with another believer who can encourage you.

4. **Stop charging and cut up your credit cards.** *"If you don't want to go into debt, don't borrow money. If you don't want to go deeper into debt, don't borrow more money"* (Larry Burkett). One-third of Americans say that having a credit card makes them more likely to make spontaneous purchases.[1]

Living debt-free involves so much more than simply paying off your credit card bills. It includes a change of lifestyle resulting in your ability to consistently live within your means. Thirty-three percent of born-again Christians say they cannot get ahead in life because of the debt they have incurred.[2]

Keep in mind that credit cards are *not* the real problem. Unrestrained spending with credit cards is the problem. So if you keep your credit cards, follow the four simple rules to resist overspending.

- Only use credit cards to purchase budgeted items.

- Gain agreement from your spouse prior to making the purchase.

- Pay your credit card bills off entirely at the end of each month.

- The first time you're unable to pay off your credit card bills, cut up the cards and don't use them again.

5. **Begin to save.** Despite a robust economy in the latter nineties, the savings rate for Americans is at the lowest level since the Great Depression — 0.5 percent.[3] That's saving $5.00 for every $1,000 earned. Even if you can only save a small amount, begin the practice of setting money aside. Don't make the mistake of waiting to get everything paid off before you begin to save.

    Without an emergency surplus account, unexpected expenses — car repairs, sick children, house repairs — invariably occur. That's when most people typically reach for credit cards. The ideal goal is to have between three to six months of your net income set aside for emergency surplus. *"You can't squeeze blood from a turnip"* goes the saying. True. If you're struggling just to pay monthly bills, it's hard to figure a way to start saving. But in order to make both tithing and saving a priority, you will likely have to cut back your lifestyle.

6. **Reduce your food costs.** Most families can cut back food expenses by cooking and eating meals at home. The average American family has the following eating patterns.

- We spend $35.50 a week to purchase food at restaurants.

- Ninety-eight percent of American households ate out in the previous month.

- As affluence grows, so does the temptation to eat out more often: one in five say they eat out more than they did last year.

- Households with children and working mothers eat out more often than average. Young, college-educated professionals also typically eat out more often than average. "Fast and convenient" are essentials for busy Americans.[4]

Reduce food expenditures by cooking in bulk — preparing multiple meals at one time, and freezing portions for future use, and by eating leftovers. That may not sound too appetizing, but remember that we're *aggressively* looking for ways to reduce monthly expenses. Don't forget to use coupons from newspapers and magazines, and shop a variety of grocery stores to find temporary bargains.

7. **Develop a schedule to repay outstanding debts.** It's unlikely that you got into debt overnight; neither will you get out of debt overnight. Suppose you owe a

How to Get Out of Debt

total of $12,000 on five credit cards. Forget paying interest for a moment. If you changed your lifestyle to pay $100 a month on the balances, and never, ever charged another thing on the cards, it would take you ten years to pay off those balances. Another way to think of it, had you started paying on those balances when George Bush first became president in 1989, you would have just now finished paying off those debts. And these calculations don't include interest!

To accelerate paying off your debts, follow this strategy.

- Focus on the account that charges the highest rate of interest, yet has the lowest balance due. Make minimum payments on all other accounts and concentrate paying all you can on this one account.

- When that account is paid off, *close it*, and roll what you were paying on it onto the next account with highest interest and lowest balance. For instance, suppose you are able to pay $75 a month to close out your Visa account first. The next account charging the highest interest and lowest balance due is Mastercard. Once Visa is paid, add the $75 you were paying Visa to your new target: the Mastercard bill.

- Continue eliminating one account at a time until each is paid off and closed.

- This strategy is only effective if you stop making charges on the account.

For further assistance in organizing a debt repayment plan, take one of the two following steps.

- Meet with a volunteer Christian financial counselor (such as those trained by Christian Financial Concepts[5]). He or she will help you organize a plan for repaying your debts, taking the steps necessary to creating and living on a budget.

- Call Consumer Credit Counseling Service of Atlanta at 1-888-771-HOPE. A credit counseling service can help you by structuring a debt repayment plan that is realistic and manageable. They do this by directly intervening with your creditors to negotiate lower monthly payments and to reduce, and sometimes eliminate, accruing interest charges.

- Both of these resources are invaluable since it is difficult to begin waging the war against debt alone. Indeed, wise King Solomon once stated, *"Two are better than one, because they have a good return for their work. If one falls down, his friend can help him up. But pity the man who falls and has no one to help him up!"* (Ecclesiastes 4:9-10).

8. **Liquidate small assets.** One of the best ways to jump-start a debt repayment plan is by selling off items around the house that you're no longer using. Most people do this by hosting a yard or garage sale to sell unused items clogging closets and garages. A successful sale may require four to six weeks of planning, depending on how much preparation time is afforded by your weekly schedule. Basically you will need time to go through every room in the house (especially closets).

- Look for items that haven't been used in the last year. If there's not a specific reason to keep it, add it to your sale pile.

- Plan your sale for the first Saturday after the first of the month. Most people receive some type of income on the first of the month.

- Plan low-cost ways to advertise your sale. Some communities have free, call-in community announcements on local radio stations. Consider making signs with large lettering. Your sale will not be well attended if no one knows you are having it!

- One caution: In your zeal to raise quick cash, be sure you don't sell items you really need, and will only have to replace by spending more money. And remember that you can only realistically do this about once a year.

9. **Liquidate large assets in an emergency.** Your particular situation may be so critical that you have to consider selling major items such as your house or a car. Those are sobering possibilities, but a genuine crisis may require unusual and more dramatic actions. For that reason, it will be wise to first meet with a trained financial counselor or seasoned business-person from your church to help you evaluate your situation.

A man's take-home pay was about $2,000 a month, and the combination of his first and second mortgage exceeded $1,300 a month, or two-thirds of his income. Every month he and his wife were depleting savings to make ends meet. We advised him to consider selling the house, getting out from under his debt load, and purchasing a home again when he could afford it.

No one likes to think about selling a home, but it was just a matter of time until this man defaulted on his mortgage, and he would have lost his home anyway.

It's not uncommon to see young newlyweds face decisions like the one below immediately after marriage. While single, young men and women typically choose to purchase nice automobiles that come with a hefty monthly payment — in the range of $300 to $400 a month is not unusual. Sporty cars driven by drivers under age 25 draw a high monthly insurance payment, perhaps another couple of hundred dollars a month. Add to that the cost of gas, and the automobile budget could easily approach $600-700 a month. Multiply that by two people just married, and the new couple may be looking at paying upwards of $1400 a month in the automobile budget. What was affordable prior to marriage may become unreasonable after marriage. And the two may be immediately faced with selling a car, or unloading a lease, which is even more difficult.

10. **It is critical to adopt a stewardship mentality in life.** All our resources — our incomes, health, automobiles, and houses — all belong to God. *"The Lord gave and the Lord has taken away; may the name of the Lord be blessed"* (Job 1:21). You can break the emotional attachment to things by realizing they belong to the Lord, and He certainly can do as He chooses with them.

Don't be afraid to take a step back today, especially if that is your only viable alternative. God may choose to humble you today and exalt you again at some point in the future. Just do what you must do today and trust God for your future. Once you yield control over the future to God, He will flood you with His peace. It is nothing less than a huge step of faith to relinquish ownership of material goods — especially big ones like houses, cars, and property. But then, Hebrews 11:6 teaches that *"Without faith it is impossible to please God."* That being true, don't be surprised when God allows the circumstances to develop in your life that require faith from you.

1 *USA Today* Snapshot Archives, 3/5/99

2 www.barna.org/PageStats.htm (8/5/98)

3 Robert J. Samuelson, "Hell No, We Won't Save!" *Washington Post,* 2/17/99, A-17

4 *Restaurants and Institutions* Magazine, 2/1/98, www.rimag.com

5 Locate a counselor in your vicinity by calling Christian Financial Concepts at 1-800-722-1976.

How Much
Is Enough?

Resource Material
for Leaders

- Leader's Guide
- Discussion/Listening Guide

How Much Is Enough?

Leader's Guide

How Much Is Enough? is a small-group process designed to help Christians know and do God's will regarding stewardship of what God has entrusted to them in all aspects of their lives. This Leader's Guide provides step-by-step guidance for facilitating group studies of the four sessions that follow each week's study. By studying this Guide, you will learn how to best implement this process in the lives of members.

The Process of How Much Is Enough?

The *How Much Is Enough?* study employs an interactive-learning process. Each day, for five days a week, members are expected to study a segment of the material and complete activities that relate to what they just read. Each day's work requires 20 to 30 minutes of study time. On Days 6 and 7 of the *Devotional Guide* (designed to be completed on weekends), no interactive work is furnished.

At the end of the week's study, members gather for group sessions. The sessions help members reflect on the concepts and experiences in *How Much Is Enough?* and apply the ideas to their lives.

Although persons may benefit from completing the studies totally on their own, without a group experience, they will have missed the critical element Jesus' disciples experienced: relationships with one another in Christ's presence. As members share their own testimonies about growing in stewardship, others give feedback and are encouraged in their own challenges and victories. Therefore, individuals are highly urged to connect with other believers to study this material.

How Much Is Enough?

Steps for Using How Much Is Enough? in Your Church

1. *Pray.* Seek God's direction about whether a study of *How Much Is Enough?* is appropriate for your church.

2. *Seek approval.* If you are a church staff member, discuss your proposal with your pastor, fellow staff members, deacon body, pertinent committees, or whatever approval process exists in your church. If you are a lay person, consult with your pastor or appropriate church staff member before scheduling a study of *How Much Is Enough?* Provide the pastor and/or staff member with copies of the *Devotional Guide,* which includes the Leader's Guide and Discussion/Listening Guide. Help church leaders understand the process, course goals, content, and procedures. Show the pastor or staff member segments of the *How Much Is Enough? Video.* Refer to the steps a church can take for a full-scale launch of the *How Much Is Enough?* emphasis (see page 117 to order *Training Kit*).

3. *Select leaders and provide training.* Use the section "How to Train Leaders" on page 122 in this Leader's Guide to train persons to lead *How Much Is Enough?* discussion groups. Refer to the section "Who can lead a *How Much Is Enough?* discussion group?" on page 118, as you recruit persons to lead.

4. *Set a time, date, and place.* The optimal time for *How Much Is Enough?* discussion groups to meet is outside the typical church schedule. If you are scheduling these sessions on the church calendar, strive for a different time than any normally-scheduled activity. Consider the possibility of a weeknight (other than traditional Wednesday-night activities), a weekday for those who are available to participate, a Saturday, or a Sunday afternoon between morning and evening worship. However, if such a plan is not possible because no other time is available, you may adapt the leader material for any

setting — discipleship training, Wednesday night prayer meeting, or even a Sunday-morning Bible study.

5. *Recruit members.* Schedule at least a four-week period to register members and promote the group. Promote this study through announcements in church publications, displays on bulletin boards, displays around the church, bulletin inserts and posters provided in the *How Much Is Enough? Training Kit*, and through testimonies in worship services, Bible-study classes, and discipleship groups. Show brief segments of the *Video*, if appropriate. Make certain each group you enlist contains no more than 10 people. If groups are larger than 10, each member may not have an opportunity to participate each week. Strive for homogeneity in groups, if possible. For example, a group formed of all retirement-age persons, or all young married couples, or all singles, would be optimal, although groups featuring a variety of ages and life circumstances can be effective as well.

If your church elects to study *How Much Is Enough?* in a large-group setting, such as in a joint assembly, strive to form small groups among the participants (10 or fewer) for discussion time. You may decide to show *Video* segments to the assembly as a whole and then ask participants to cluster in small discussion groups throughout the meeting area. Supply trained leaders for each group.

6. *Order materials.* At least six weeks in advance of the starting date, order one Devotional Guide for each participant. If a couple participates, order individual books for both the husband and wife. *How Much Is Enough?* resources with item numbers include:

- *How Much Is Enough? Devotional Guide*   (0-7673-9559-X)
- *How Much Is Enough? Training Kit*   (0-7673-9560-3)
- *How Much Is Enough? Video*   (0-7673-9563-8)
- *How Much Is Enough? Poster*   (0-7673-9562-X)
- *How Much Is Enough? Bulletin Insert*   (0-7673-9561-1)

How Much Is Enough?

7. ***Set fees.*** Unless the church has decided to subsidize the cost, ask members to purchase their own books. Members should pay at least part of the cost to invest in ***How Much Is Enough?***

8. ***Determine child care.*** Decide whether you will provide child care for group members' children. Child care will allow some persons to participate who could not otherwise do so. Ideally the church can offer this as a complimentary service to members, if the meetings are held at a time during the week when child care is not normally provided for church activities. However, the church could also arrange child care for a fee as well.

9. ***Get started.*** Read the Leader's Guide, read the Discussion/Listening Guide, watch all *Video* segments, and complete the *Devotional Guide* yourself before attempting to lead the study. Work at least one week ahead of the group you lead. For example, before you conduct the Week 1 session, be sure you have studied up through the Week 2 devotionals, completed the interactive material, and watched the corresponding *Video* segments so you can give members any special instructions necessary for the following week's study.

How to Lead a Small Group

1. ***Who can lead a How Much Is Enough? discussion group?*** Any church member, either a layperson or church staff member, can lead the group. A person may resist leading a group on this topic because he or she may think, "I'm still struggling in the area of finances. I want to do things in a thoroughly Christ-centered way, but I'm not there yet." The ideal leader is a fellow struggler — someone who relates to the issues involved and who is perhaps just a little farther down the road than the rest of his or her group members in terms of surrendering every aspect of stewardship to God's control. An ideal gro p leader is

How Much Is Enough?

someone who has a burden on his or her heart regarding proper stewardship of all resources, financial and otherwise, and who can share transparently from his or her own experiences. Since the group leader leads by modeling, recruiting leaders who are role models in terms of giving their time, talents, and energies for the Lord's work is important. Assure leaders you recruit that the Discussion/Listening Guide provides detailed instruction for how to lead the group.

2. *What are some traits of an effective group leader?* This person . . .

   - Is a growing Christian, a person of prayer, and one who has faith in what God can do.

   - Has a commitment to keep confidential information private.

   - Is an active member of the sponsoring church.

   - Is able to relate well to people.

   - Has a knowledge of Scripture.

   - Senses God's call to be involved in a ministry of financial restoration.

   - Is comfortable in the presence of people who share painful life experiences. In the process of these group discussions, members may reflect on hurtful times when they have made wrong choices about spending money, spending time with family, and spending time with God. A person who only feels comfortable when contemporaries are cheerful and upbeat may need to reconsider whether he or she is appropriate to lead a *How Much Is Enough?* group.

3. *What are some skills that a group leader needs?* A successful group leader for *How Much Is Enough?* will . . .

   - Maintain eye contact as members share. When appropriate, nod your head or use occasional verbal phrases to indicate that you are listening to what someone is saying.

Leader's Guide

How Much Is Enough?

- Use good listening skills. To encourage sharing, make sure you or someone in the group offers some type of response when any group member shares.

- Try to read body language and nonverbal cues. Attempt to draw out people who are, for example, listening intently, withdrawing, or looking as though they are full of pain. Depend on God for sensitivity.

- Affirm strong emotion, such as tears. Phrases like "I sense a lot of hurt in what you just shared . . . " or "I'm sure that must have been very disappointing" help people put a name to their emotions and validate them.

- Avoid allowing one member to dominate discussions. If someone has talked too long, gently try to steer the conversation to someone else. Help the person summarize. Watch for the slightest break in monologue to turn the conversation to someone else. State, "I'm wondering whether anyone else has a thought to share on this subject."

- Steer the group away from advice-giving. Help members share out of their own experience ("Something that has worked for me is . . ." or "Here's what I've learned . . .") instead of prefacing remarks with, "What you should do is . . . "

4. *Arranging the room for learning.* Use the following ideas to make the room arrangement and physical environment aid the group process:

- Arrange chairs in a circle so members can see each other face to face. Keep chairs relatively close together.

- Place in the circle only enough chairs to seat members who attend the session. If you know of absences already, withdraw that number of chairs from the circle. If someone fails to show up by the time the group starts, withdraw that person's chair.

How Much Is Enough?

- Remove any unnecessary items in the room. Groups work best when chairs are free of tables and members are seated in circle without any distractions in front of them.

- Position training equipment, such a television monitor, so that all members can see without difficulty.

5. *Set guidelines for healthy group life.*

- Announce to the group that you will begin and end on time. Begin the group even if all members have not arrived. Conclude at the designated hour. Sometimes group members have not experienced consistency and proper boundaries of any type in their lives; this may have contributed to their financial chaos. Any consistency you demonstrate may help them realize that they, too, can operate from a sense of orderliness. If a member arrives late, continue the group process matter-of-factly and without undue attention to the tardiness. If necessary, you might say to the latecomer, briefly, "We were discussing the fact that . . . ."

- Ask members to avoid bringing drinks, candy, mints, or gum to group meetings. These items can distract from an atmosphere conducive to sharing.

- Provide a box of tissue at each group meeting. Position it on the floor in the center of the room. Instruct members to feel free to take a tissue if they need one. Providing tissues helps demonstrate to members that this is a "safe place" to express emotions. Ask members to take their own tissue and to refrain from passing it to others, unless someone is physically incapacitated. Shoving a tissue in front of someone who is shedding tears can distract the person from sharing.

- Ask members to agree to confidentiality—what is said in the group remains in the group. (A pledge to confidentiality is included in

Leader's Guide

How Much Is Enough?

the Covenant which members will be asked to sign in group session 1. See page 6 of this *Devotional Guide*.)

- Ask members to let you, as leader, know in advance if they realize they must miss a session. Advise members to make up any session missed by arranging a time to meet with you privately before the next meeting to review material covered during the session.

How a How Much Is Enough? Group Session Works

1. Each group session is one hour in length. Time increments for each segment of the session are provided in the Discussion/Listening Guide.

2. Members complete all weekly assignments before the group sessions.

3. The first part of the session involves processing the week's devotional material and interactive material. In the second part of the meeting, the leader shows *Video* segments illustrating real-life situations involving money and other stewardship matters; group members discuss what they observe on the *Video*.

4. Allow for prayer time at the end. Invite prayer requests, particularly those that involve money matters. Also invite praises for victories achieved in stewardship areas.

How to Train Leaders

1. Churches that elect to study *How Much Is Enough?* in a churchwide emphasis can benefit from conducting a leader training several weeks before the study. After leaders are enlisted, ask them to commit to a two-hour training session to equip them to lead *How Much Is Enough?* groups.

How Much Is Enough?

2. Ask leaders to complete week 1 of their *How Much Is Enough? Devotional Guide* before attending the training so they will be generally familiar with the concept and learning approach.

3. If you have more than 10 leaders attending the training session, divide the group and ask another facilitator to lead a separate training for one of the groups while you lead the other one.

4. Prepare the meeting room.
   * Provide a circle of chairs for the number of participants.
   * Provide a VCR and a monitor.
   * Provide pencils for participants.
   * Prepare name tags, if necessary.

5. Sample training schedule (2 hours)

   a. Introduction (15 minutes)
   Ask participants to introduce themselves to each other if they are not well acquainted. Ask each participant to tell one struggle and one victory he or she has experienced in the area of personal stewardship (time, talents, other resources).

   b. Describe the plan for the *How Much Is Enough?* studies in your church (15 minutes).

   Explain the rationale for the church's scheduling the emphasis, the biblical basis, the benefits to the individual church member, and the benefits to the church as a corporate body. Overview the plans that are being made for church preparation (including the launch, if scheduled), promotion, enlistment, child care, fees, scheduling.

   c. Review the high points of the section "How to Lead a Small Group" on page 118 of this Leader's Guide. Invite questions (15 minutes).

How Much Is Enough?

d. Review the *Devotional Guide* design and how to use it (10 minutes). Explain that the interactive style of the material allows members to read the *Devotional Guide* and then answer the questions that relate to the material members just read. Explain that in some situations, members are ask to fulfill an assignment, such as praying with a prayer partner, removing themselves to a quiet place to meditate, share a verse with another person, etc. Discuss questions or comments participants have.

e. Show the *Video* and Lead in Discussion (45 minutes)
    Show one or two *Video* segments that accompany each week of the ***How Much Is Enough?*** study (approximately 15 minutes each). Ask participants to make notes or write questions as they watch the *Video* segments. Lead a group discussion of the *Video* segments. Ask members to discuss the life situations the vignettes present. Ask participants to describe times they have found themselves in similar dilemmas as the individuals depicted in the vignettes. Use the Discussion/Listening Guide material that corresponds with each *Video* segment. Discuss ways to provide and use *Videotapes* for multiple groups. For example, a church could stagger meeting times of groups so that several groups could share a *Video*. The church may also acquire multiple copies of the *Video*.

f. Explain leadership follow-up meetings of the ***How Much Is Enough?*** emphasis (15 minutes).

    (1) Schedule a meeting of all the leaders after the Week 1, small-group session. The meeting will allow leaders to debrief, compare experiences, ask questions, and encourage each other.

    (2) Explain plans for a Celebration Sunday.

    (3) Explain whether the church plans to provide for new study groups after the ***How Much Is Enough?*** emphasis is complete.

g. Lead the group leaders in conversational prayer for the upcoming groups (5 minutes).

Pray for growth in the lives of individual members and in the life of the church through the *How Much Is Enough?* study.

A Key Decision

How Much Is Enough? was written with the assumption that members have already received Jesus Christ as their Savior and Lord. However, participants possibly may realize as they study that they have never invited Christ into their lives. Be alert to this possibility. Guidance on how to receive Christ appears in the *Devotional Guide*, pages 48-49. Be available to answer questions for members who accept Christ when they reach this point in the study. Arrange for them to talk to a pastor or other church leader. You may want to give them a copy of *Survival Kit: Five Keys to Effective Spiritual Growth* (0-8054-9770-6), available from the Customer Service Center, 127 Ninth Avenue, North; Nashville, TN 37234; 1-800-458-2772.

How Much Is Enough?

Discussion/Listening Guide

BEFORE EACH SESSION

❑ Read the Leader's Guide material on "How to Lead a Small Group" to refresh your memory on how to conduct group sessions.

❑ Be sure you have completed all the learning activities for the week of *How Much Is Enough?* that your group is studying. Preview the *Video* segment that corresponds to the session you are about to lead. Cue up the *Video* so this particular segment is ready to show.

❑ **Option:** Review and evaluate the comedy sketch that preceeds each group discussion. Determine if the comedy sketch is appropriate for your small group.

❑ Stay a week ahead of the group at all times. Before each group session, complete the learning activities for the following week's work of *How Much Is Enough?* so you can be ready to answer questions or give specific directions.

❑ Find a quiet time and place to pray for group members by name. Ask the Lord to give you the wisdom you need to prepare for and lead the session that is ahead.

❑ If you are meeting in a home, check with the host and/or hostess to be sure he or she is prepared for the group this week.

❑ Arrange in a circle only enough chairs for everyone attending.

❑ For group session 1, secure enough name tags (ideally, the permanent variety, so you can reuse the outer casings) for those you expect to

How Much Is Enough?

attend. Collect name tags at the end of each session and make them available as members arrive each week.

❏ Arrange for a VCR and monitor to show the *Video* during the group session.

❏ Plan to stay within the times given for each activity. However, allowing members to share freely is far more important than sticking legalistically to a plan you develop for the group session. Group members sometimes arrive at a session eager to tell about something that happened in their lives related to that week's content. Be sensitive to this need, and be flexible. Allow God to work in your group.

GROUP SESSION 1

DURING THE SESSION *(1 hour)*

PART 1 — DISCUSSING WEEK 1 *(35 minutes)*

1. Welcome each person. Invite each person to make a name tag.

2. Begin promptly. Remind the group that you will begin and end each session on time. If group members want to fellowship or have additional discussions after the sessions, they may do so, but they can count on you to be prompt.

3. Ask each member to briefly share one of their "if onlys" from their Day 1 work. Ask members to share one statement they wrote about things they wish they could change in their lives. *(For example: "I'd be happy with myself if only I owned a vacation home.")* After all have shared, tell members you hope the lesson impressed on them the fact that what we achieve or own or how we look doesn't determine who we are.

How Much Is Enough?

4. Invite members to share ways they believe God has created them uniquely. Ask each person to name one way he or she responded to the Day 1 question, "What are some of the unique contributions you have to make to life?"

5. As leader, give a brief testimony about your own experience with having a daily quiet time. *(For example, a leader might tell about how he has developed the practice of private prayer and Bible study while his co-workers take coffee breaks.)* Then call on a volunteer to give his or her testimony.

6. One-to-one: Ask members to pair up for two minutes to discuss ways each is striving to increase his/her time spent in God's Word. *(When pairing up members for activities, encourage husbands and wives to always form a pair, if you have couples in the group.)*

7. Invite a testimony about a time in which a member has seen how God, through answered prayer, has shown how concerned He is with the details of his or her life. Affirm for members the fact that God is interested in the details of our financial stewardship, as well, and that He is available to help them bring this in line with His guidelines.

8. Ask a couple of members to report their experience of spending time with a family member, sharing various aspects of their spiritual life, as their Day 4 work requested.

9. Call on a volunteer to say aloud 1 John 1:9 after memorizing it. Divide the large group into two smaller groups. (If you have more than 10 persons in your large group, make sure that no small group has more than four or five members.) Ask each person in the small groups to share a wrong choice that he or she has made in the area of money management. After each person in the small group has shared, ask one person in each group to lead a prayer, thanking God that He forgives our shortcomings and asking Him to help all members make changes in this area.

Discussion/Listening Guide
How Much Is Enough?

PART 2 — DISCUSSING THE *VIDEO* *(20 minutes)*

1. Tell group members, "Let's listen to how Larry Burkett and a small group discuss some of the concepts from your Week 1 work."

2. Show *Video* segment.

3. Choose from among these questions to discuss with your group, based on what they observed in the *Video*.

   • In the *Video*, Larry speaks of his decision to "resign as manager of the universe" — being overly responsible for everything — in his effort to set priorities. Ask members to share about times in which their desire to be "super responsible" has kept them from spending time with the Lord.

   • Remind members that Larry described his difficulties in saying "no" to Christian activities even when his plate was full. Call on a volunteer to tell how he or she deals with setting priorities in this area.

   • Ask group members to respond to Larry's statement that he sometimes wonders whether a person has ever trusted Christ as Lord and Savior in the first place if that person doesn't give to God and spend time in the Word.

   • In the *Video*, Larry says we can ask ourselves, "Do I really trust God, or have I just been saying I trust God?" Ask a group member to testify about a time when he or she merely gave lip service to trusting God. Then ask someone to share about a time when he or she trusted even without seeing any direct evidence of God's hand.

   • Larry spoke about his kidney surgery for cancer and stated, "One of the greatest revelations of my life was to discover that I had perfect peace" as he faced the operation. Ask a member to tell about a time when he or she experienced a kind of peace the world cannot give.

How Much Is Enough?

PART 3 — CIRCLE OF PRAYER *(5 minutes)*

1. Express gratitude that you are part of the group. Request members' prayers for you as you serve them during the weeks that follow.

2. Close in a circle of prayer. Ask members to voice one-sentence prayers for personal concerns that have been raised during the discussion. As leader, close the prayer time.

GROUP SESSION 2

DURING THE SESSION *(1 hour)*

PART 1 — DISCUSSING WEEK 2 *(35 minutes)*

1. Arrive early and fellowship with members as they arrive. Be alert and available to discuss any questions they may have. Begin on time.

2. As a get-started activity, ask each member to share one of his or her current priorities at this time in life *(from the Day 1 work)*. Remind members that a priority means that people have determined that some choices will be more important than others in their lives because of how they relate to their life goals. *(For example, if your life goal is to witness for the Lord overseas someday, your priority right now might be to save for a volunteer missions trip as a first step in that process.)*

3. Invite two volunteers to share one characteristic of their strategic, organized plan for spending. Then share a characteristic of your own plan. *(For example, your family might be in the process of cutting back from $100 to $80 per payday to be allocated for clothing expenses over a two-week period. The cutback may be due to a family goal of debt*

How Much Is Enough?

reduction.) As leader, remember to affirm members when they share about making taking positive steps.

4. Ask members to tell what specific things they do to make room in their schedule for God. Ask, "Can you see any difference in your life as a result of taking this step?"

5. Call for a testimony about how a member has learned to say "No" to people's requests when appropriate. Ask another member to recall a Scripture that gives him or her strength to say "No" when doing so is called for.

6. Divide the large group into smaller groups. No group should contain more than four or five members. Ask members within their groups to share about times they realize their family has been impacted by lack of financial goals. Ask one member from each group to pray that all members will have God's wisdom in their family financial dealings.

7. Return to the large group. Call for a volunteer to share the results of a spiritual gifts inventory he or she may have taken. Ask that person how he or she believes those gifts can be used to benefit the body of Christ.

8. Ask a couple of members to share an experience when they have experienced "iron sharpening iron," as the devotional described, as they have interacted with a group of other believers.

9. Instruct members to pair off for this activity. Within the pairs, members can share their experiences of having an accountability partner for financial stewardship. If members do not have such a person in their lives, ask the pairs to pray that a responsible person will be found to fill this role.

How Much Is Enough?

PART 2 — DISCUSSING THE VIDEO *(20 minutes)*

1. Tell group members, "Let's listen to how Larry Burkett and a small group discuss some of the concepts from your Week 2 work."

2. Show the *Video* segment.

3. Choose from among these questions to discuss with your group, based on what they observed in the *Video*.

   • Ask group members to respond to Larry's description of his budget — an instrument that doesn't reveal how much to spend but one that simply "helps me stick to the plan I've created." Ask members whether that description gives them an enhanced perspective of what a budget can accomplish.

   • In the *Video*, Larry discusses the importance of engaged couples discussing their financial goals. Ask whether anyone in the group underwent financial counseling, or spent time seriously studying their financial goals, before marriage. If so, what difference has this made in the marriage relationship?

   • Larry reminds the group that any question people have about money is answered in God's Word. Ask group members to share Scriptures that have particularly helped them in regard to money matters.

   • In the video, Larry distinguishes between using credit cards responsibly — as a substitute for cash, with bills being paid when the statement comes in — versus using them to buy something that a person can't afford to own. Call for volunteers to respond to this distinction he makes.

   • Ask for responses to Larry's comment, "I don't think you can be in financial bondage and be spiritually free." *(Example: Some people are unable to give to help others, even though they desire to, because of their discouraging financial condition.)*

133

How Much Is Enough?

PART 3 — CIRCLE OF PRAYER *(5 minutes)*

1. Thank members for their participation in this session. Remind members to pray for each other throughout the week.

2. Close in a circle of prayer. Ask members to voice one-sentence prayers of thanksgiving for something meaningful they experienced during today's group meeting.

GROUP SESSION 3

DURING THE SESSION *(1 hour)*

PART 1 — DISCUSSING WEEK 3 *(35 minutes)*

1. Begin the session on time even if all members are not present. Ask for special prayer requests. As leader, begin with a brief prayer.

2. Ask a couple of volunteers to share ways they have resisted when God prompted them to give more generously of their time, money, attention, or affection. Affirm their courage for relating these testimonies. Remind members that confessing our shortcomings and seeking God's help to improve is a sign of strength, not weakness.

3. Pair members up for the next exercise. Ask members to share within pairs one way in which their marriage has dealt with a financial conflict. If some group members are single, ask them to share a source of financial conflict they recall from their families of origin. Then call on a volunteer to share with the large group a positive step that has been taken within his or her marriage to deal with a financial difficulty.

How Much Is Enough?

4. Call on someone in the group you know may already be taking steps toward debt-free living. Ask that person to share with the group what progress has been made. Invite questions about a debt-free lifestyle.

5. Ask a volunteer to share about a time when he or she learned to speak up for a need. What was the result? Then ask a volunteer to share about a time when he or she looked for a needy person to bless. What happened in that instance?

6. Divide into small groups — no larger than four or five per group. Assign each group one of the case studies from Day 4 of the Week 3 work. Ask groups to discuss what the person in their case study needed to do to give God first place in his or her life. Call on one group to report their answer as the large group reconvenes.

7. Tell your own testimony about a time in which you were blessed because you were obedient to God in your tithing. *(For example, one leader might testify about how God provided scholarship money for her child's college expenses after the family made a commitment to continue tithing during difficult times.)* Ask another group member to share as well.

8. Ask someone to share what God might be putting on his or her heart, through this *How Much Is Enough?* study about sacrificial, financial giving to the Lord — beyond a perfunctory minimum, just to get by.

9. End this part of the session with a time of prayer. Likely this session will have involved some true confessional sharing of past mistakes and testimonies of how God may be stirring in individual hearts. Ask each group member to pray aloud briefly for the person on his or her right — that God would empower this member to be bold in the areas of victory and challenge that the person has mentioned in the discussion time.

How Much Is Enough?

PART 2 — DISCUSSING THE *VIDEO* (*20 minutes*)

1. Tell group members, "Let's listen to how Larry Burkett and a small group discuss some of the concepts from your Week 3 work."

2. Show the *Video* segment.

3. Choose from among these questions to discuss with your group, based on what they observed in the *Video*.

   • In the *Video*, Larry discussed the fact that today's society sends people the message that they're never to be content — to always want more and more things. Ask group members how they personally experience this message and how they respond to it.

   • Larry stated in the *Video*, "Once someone knows Jesus, giving flows from that." Call on members to give testimonies about whether or not this concept is true in their lives.

   • Ask members to respond to Larry's comment, "Sacrificing is giving up something you want for the needs of another." Call for testimonies about a time when members feel they genuinely purposed to give up something to meet someone else's need.

   • In the *Video*, group members discussed the tendency to sacrifice something and then say, "OK, God, what do I get in return?" Ask your group members to discuss ways they experience this tendency and how someone might counter it.

   • Ask group members to respond to Larry's statement, "Things don't last. Only God and people last," as it relates to how people invest their resources.

How Much Is Enough?

PART 3 — CLOSING PRAYER *(5 minutes)*

1. Announce the meeting time and place for next week. Encourage members to place Christ first in their lives in all areas during the week ahead.

2. Call on a volunteer to close the session in prayer, asking God's blessing on members as they study the concluding week's work.

GROUP SESSION 4

DURING THE SESSION *(1 hour)*

PART 1 — DISCUSSING WEEK 4 *(35 minutes)*

1. Begin on time and with prayer. Ask each member to share something he or she has grown to appreciate about the person seated to the left.

2. Note that this week's devotional uses the term "city without walls" in regard to lack of restraint. Ask members this question: When have you been tempted to spend as though you are a "city without walls"? Generously affirm any group member who willingly answers aloud this sensitive question.

3. Ask for two volunteers to share ways they might be feeling convicted to cut back in their lifestyle in order to save more. Share your own experience with lifestyle cutbacks in order to save. *(For example, you might tell about learning to cut your children's hair or sewing your family's clothing as a savings measure.)*

4. Pair members up to answer this question from the Day 2 work: Has your witness for Christ ever been undermined because you failed to

Discussion/Listening Guide

How Much Is Enough?

demonstrate financial responsibility? As with question 3, confessing shortcomings in this area requires much boldness. Thank members for their willingness to be transparent with each other.

5. Call for someone who has some experience with setting aside 3-6 months' income in a contingency fund to tell the group how this worked. Urge members to be open to this suggestion about an emergency fund if they do not currently make this a practice.

6. Tell your own experience about a time in which you've been the most effective at maintaining a budget. Call on another group member who is willing to share.

7. Divide into small groups of no more than four or five. Ask members to share within their group how they reacted to the devotional's urging that they use their resources to see the nations come to Christ. Ask group members to give testimonies about why missions giving is important to them. Back in the large group, call on one member to share his or her testimony with the entire group.

8. Ask someone to tell about a time when God has called him or her to a task and then supplied what was needed to perform the task. Reiterate that this has been an overriding theme of the *How Much Is Enough?* study — that God will truly provide when we are walking in the center of His will.

9. Close this discussion time by asking each member to tell briefly one change God has led him or her to make in the area of personal stewardship during the four-week study.

PART 2 — DISCUSSING THE VIDEO *(20 minutes)*

1. Tell group members, "Let's listen to how Larry Burkett and a small group discuss some of the concepts from your Week 4 work."

2. Show the *Video* segment.

3. Choose from among these questions to discuss with your group, based on what they observed in the *Video*.

   • Ask a member to restate the distinction the *Video* makes between faith and presumption. Ask someone to give his or her reaction to Larry's statement, "Faith is where I trust God for something that I know is in His will for me but I'm unable to do for myself."

   • Ask for someone's response to Larry's comment, "One day when we stand in heaven, we will see what stewardship is all about." Ask group members what changes that concept might prompt them to make in their use of resources?

   • Note that Larry suggests that parents teach by example when they educate their children about giving. Ask members to share about a time when their children saw them giving sacrificially.

   • In the *Video*, a group member testifies that her husband took a cut in pay when he accepted a job requiring less travel so that he could spend more time with their children. Call for testimonies from members who may have made similar decisions or life adjustments.

   • Note that Larry specifies that God's Word does not *prohibit* Christians from borrowing money; it only *controls* their borrowing. Ask group members to recall the three scriptural conditions Larry cites for borrowing. *(Borrowing ought to be rare, it ought to be short-term, and it should never involve a surety—taking on an obligation that one doesn't have certain means of repaying.)*

Notes

How Much Is Enough?

PART 3 — CLOSING PRAYER *(5 minutes)*

1. Discuss any plans that members might have for follow-up study or for participating in the celebration Sunday that your church may schedule to conclude the *How Much Is Enough?* study. Express appreciation to the members for their participation in the group. Assure them you will continue to pray for them. Offer to be available for them as needs arise.

2. Ask members to conclude their time together with a circle of prayer. As leader, pray that God will help all members be faithful in the areas of personal stewardship where they have committed to work.

Listening Guide

How Much Is Enough?

Notes

CHRISTIAN GROWTH STUDY PLAN

Preparing Christians to Serve

In the **Christian Growth Study Plan (formerly Church Study Course),** this book *HOW MUCH IS ENOUGH? 30 DAYS TO PERSONAL REVIVAL* is a resource for course credit in the subject area **STEWARDSHIP** of the Christian Growth category of diploma plans. To receive credit, read the book, complete the learning activities, show your work to your pastor, a staff member or church leader, then complete the information on the next page. The form may be duplicated. Send the completed page to:

Christian Growth Study Plan
127 Ninth Avenue, North, MSN 117
Nashville, TN 37234-0117
FAX: (615)251-5067

For information about the Christian Growth Study Plan, refer to the current Christian Growth Study Plan Catalog. Your church office may have a copy. If not, request a free copy from the Christian Growth Study Plan office (615/251-2525).

HOW MUCH IS ENOUGH? 30 DAYS TO PERSONAL REVIVAL

COURSE NUMBER: CG- 0500

PARTICIPANT INFORMATION

Social Security Number (USA Only)

| | - | | | - | | | | |

Personal CGSP Number*

| | - | | | | - | | | |

Date of Birth (Mo., Day, Yr.)

| | - | | - | | |

Name (First, MI, Last)

☐Mr. ☐Miss
☐Mrs. ☐

Address (Street, Route, or P.O. Box)

City, State, or Province

Home Phone | | | - | | | |

Zip/Postal Code | | | | | |

CHURCH INFORMATION

Church Name

Address (Street, Route, or P.O. Box)

City, State, or Province

Zip/Postal Code

CHANGE REQUEST ONLY

☐Former Name

City, State, or Province

Zip/Postal Code

☐Former Address

City, State, or Province

Zip/Postal Code

☐Former Church

City, State, or Province

Zip/Postal Code

Signature of Pastor, Conference Leader, or Other Church Leader

Date

*New participants are requested but not required to give SS# and date of birth. Existing participants, please give CGSP# when using SS# for the first time.
Thereafter, only one ID# is required. *Mail To:* Christian Growth Study Plan, 127 Ninth Ave., North, MSN 117, Nashville, TN 37234-0117. Fax: (615)251-5067